T0266725

Michigan
BY THEME
DAY TRIPS

Kathryn Houghton
prior edition by Mike Link and Kate Crowley

Adventure Publications
Cambridge, Minnesota

Safety Notice Michigan has natural hazards such as bluffs and drop-offs, as well as potentially danger-ous animals including black bears and, less commonly, rattlesnakes. Always heed posted safety warnings, take commonsense safety precautions, and remain aware of your surroundings. You're responsible for your own safety.

For the latest information about destinations in this book that have been affected by the coronavirus, please check the phone numbers and websites in the trip profiles. For news and updates about the corona virus in Michigan, see michigan.gov/coronavirus.

For additional Michigan Day Trips, visit Ron Rademacher's excellent website, www.michiganbackroads.com

Editors: Brett Ortler and Ritchey Halphen
Cover and book design by Jonathan Norberg

Front cover photo: Big Sable Point Lighthouse, Ludington, MI: **Jack R Perry Photography/shutterstock. com** map: **Globe Turner/shutterstock.com**
Back cover photo: **Lattasit Laohasiriwong/shutterstock.com**

Interior photos by **Mike Link** except:
Page 215 by **Kathryn Houghton**
Photos used under license from Shutterstock.com:

Agami Photo Agency: 25; Arken_bob: 113; Becky Swora: 20; carl ballou: 94; cindylindowphotography: 196; Courtney Tomlinson: 161; Craig Sterken: 81, 179, 185; Doug Lemke: 131; Edgar Lee Espe: 155; ehrlif: 165; Ezume Images: 186; Gary Paul Lewis: 198; Gary R Ennis Photos: 192; Ivan Cholakov: 151; iyd39: 195; John McCormick: 9; Jon Bilous: 34; Kenneth Keifer: 89; lphoto: 93; MaxyM: 103; McKeeDigital: 65; MILA Zed: 71; Oleksandr Koretskyi: 49; Pictureguy: 5; PQK: 37; SNEHIT PHOTO: 59; Steven Schremp: 122; techwiseguy: 145; Todd Maertz: 176; Victoria L. Asgaard: 182

This image is licensed under the Attribution 2.0 Generic (CC BY 2.0) license, which is available at https://creativecommons.org/licenses/by/2.0/: **Jeremy Thompson**: 43, "Crystal Mountain 001", original image via https://flickr.com/photos/rollercoasterphilosophy/7903563992

This image is licensed under the CC0 1.0 Universal (CC0 1.0) Public Domain Dedication license, which is available at https://creativecommons.org/publicdomain/zero/1.0/: **Gary Todd**: 168; **Terry Atwell, Air Force**: 146; **Wwoods, US Navy**: 173

10 9 8 7 6 5

Michigan Day Trips by Theme
Third Edition
Copyright © 2021 by Kathryn Houghton; copyright © 2013 and 2016 by Mike Link and Kate Crowley
Adventure Publications
An imprint of AdventureKEEN
310 Garfield Street South
Cambridge, Minnesota 55008
(800) 678-7006
www.adventurepublications.net
All rights reserved
Printed in China
ISBN 978-1-59193-975-7 (pbk.); ISBN. 978-1-59193-976-4 (ebook)

Table of Contents

Dedication

To all the people who, like me, call this wonderful state home.

—Kathryn Houghton

To Kate, who makes all my travel better.

—Mike Lin

Acknowledgments

Thanks to all the business owners, workers, and customers who took time out of their pandemic quarantine to answer my questions.

—K. H

I would like to thank Pure Michigan for the great work they do in publicizing the assets of Michigan. I am also thankful for the great hospitality of the people who live along the shore of Lake Superior and greeted Kate and me as we walked by. Finally, I'd like to thank the Great Lakes themselves, which give Michigan so much of its beauty and deserve better care and protection.

—M.

Authors' Note

Some day trips in this book require buying the **Michigan Recreation Passport,** a parking/day-use pass. Check michigan.gov/recreationpassport for more information, including details on pricing.

Whitefish Point Light Station

Traverse City Trail

MICHIGAN IS A MAGNIFICENT place for the outdoor adventurer. Four of the Great Lakes touch the state's borders, so there are unlimited opportunities for sailing, boating, kayaking, canoeing, or fishing. But Michigan's outdoor opportunities are not restricted to the Great Lakes, as endless inland adventures await as well. Michigan is ideal for hiking, backpacking, and biking. Whatever adventure you choose, Michigan is a state where staying fit is as easy as stepping outside and into nature.

OUTDOOR ADVENTURES

(continued on next page)

esque Isle River, Porcupine Mountains Wilderness State Park

1 Au Sable National Scenic River

Huron-Manistee National Forests M-33 in Mio to Forest Service Road 4001 in Curran just above Alcona Pond
tinyurl.com/ausablescenicriver

There is nothing like floating down a river, and the Au Sable is world-class. The 22-mile free-flowing section, federally designated as a National Scenic River, is superb and travels through national forests that are home to a variety of wildlife, including Kirtland's warbler and the Karner blue butterfly. The river itself has trout, bass, and walleye. With nearby outfitters who can provide gear and shuttles and a road paralleling the river, there are many options for a day trip or for even longer adventures.

2 Bangor to South Haven Heritage Water Trail

Bangor trailhead   North Center Street (0.25 mile north of MI-43), Bangor 49013

South Haven trailhead   South Haven Municipal Marina South, 345 Water St., South Haven 49090
tinyurl.com/bangorsouthhavenwatertrail

On this water trail, birdsong and greenery will be your constant companions. Watch for bald eagles, wild turkeys, spotted sandpipers, great crested flycatchers, and a variety of other species. Though the 21-mile-long water trail has had a reputation for wild and overgrown areas with overhanging branches and downed trees, a multiyear project is focusing on making the entire waterway passable for canoeists. In addition, the project has installed more than a dozen interpretive signs along the route. Check the website above for the most up-to-date information.

3 Battle Creek Linear Park

Multiple trailheads in Battle Creek; see map at website below
bcparks.org/134/linear-park

In addition to fishing, picnic areas, and playgrounds for the kids, Battle Creek Linear Park has six paved loops ranging from 1 to 10.5 miles long—more than 26 miles in all. Whether you want to take an easy stroll or get in a vigorous jog, you're sure to find the path that's right for you. Here, you can also learn about the plants, animals, and history of the Battle Creek area.

Copper Harbor Bike Trails

Multiple trails in Copper Harbor; see website below for an interactive map
copperharbortrails.org/trails

Mountain bikers are a special breed: instead of flat paved trails and easy routes, they want obstacle-laden trails with mixed grades and plenty of challenges. Copper Harbor is home to more than 37 miles of forested trails offering these things and more. If that's not enough, the views will take your breath away (whatever breath you have left after making your way up the steep grades, that is). If anything can match Lake Superior's ruggedness, this is it. The Copper Harbor Trails system has a variety of difficulty levels, from easy trails for the beginner to black-diamond trails for the expert. Most trails are open to hikers, too. A shuttle service is available to the more remote trailheads.

Eben Ice Caves

Frey Road, Deerton 49822
facebook.com/ebenicecaves

Also known as the Rock River Canyon Ice Caves, these cave-like structures of ice form when melting snow runs over a cliff and freezes in stalactites. This makes the ice caves very weather-dependent, but it also ensures that no two trips will ever be the same. The caves are located in Hiawatha National Forest, and parking is available; the total walk from your car to the caves will likely be less than a mile. Come prepared for hiking on slippery snow and ice surfaces, as there are no equipment rentals at the site.

Falling Waters Trail

Eastern trailhead 3714 Weatherwax Drive, Jackson 49203

Western trailhead River Street just north of Coxon Street (just before the trestle bridge over the North Branch Kalamazoo River), Concord 49202
co.jackson.mi.us/1218/falling-waters-trail

The Rails-to-Trails Conservancy has a willing partner in the State of Michigan, and their collaboration has resulted in some of the best biking options in the country. This 10.5-mile trail is just one example of what Michigan has to offer. It follows the railroad bed of the former Michigan Central Railroad, and runners, walkers, in-line skaters, and bikers will find an easy and pleasurable route that passes forests, flowers, wetlands, fields, and rural landscapes. One highlight of the trail is where it cuts straight across Lime Lake.

The trail takes its name from the Potawatomi Indians, who called the area "the land of falling waters." Learn more about the history of the area at nearby Falling Waters Trail County Park.

10-11 Multiple access points

7 Fred Meijer White Pine Trail State Park

Southern trailhead West River Drive NE at Lamoreaux Drive NE, Comstock Park 49321

Northern trailhead West Chapin Street at South Lake Street, Cadillac 49601
whitepinetrail.com

At 92 miles, this is the state's longest rail-to-trail conversion. Most of the trail is paved, and work is underway to update the remaining sections of gravel. Like all good trails, this one can be used for many purposes: hiking, running, biking, and skating in the summer and skiing and snowmobiling in the winter. The trail itself is a leisurely trek with few slopes and a comforting rural landscape dotted with more than a dozen small towns. This trail was named in honor of Frederik Meijer, a Michigan-born businessman who invested in many trails around the state. Its name also honors the white pine, the official state tree.

8 Hart-Montague Trail State Park

Southern trailhead Spring Street, about one block east of Water Street, Montague 49437

Northern trailhead West Polk Road, about 0.8 mile east of US 31, Hart 49420
tinyurl.com/hartmontaguetrail

This 22-mile trail was an early addition to Michigan's rail-trails system, which is now envied nationwide. Located in Oceana and Muskegon Counties, this park features charming scenery that includes farms and silos, meadows, birds and flowers, remnant forests, and a combination of scenic overlooks and small towns. Plan to dine in a local restaurant, treat yourself to ice cream, and return over the same route—you'll be surprised by how different the journey back looks.

9 Headlands International Dark Sky Park

15675 Headlands Road, Mackinaw City 49701
midarkskypark.org

Visit this park during the day for hiking, wildlife viewing, and cross-country skiing: this is a good spot for the aspiring nature photographer. But unlike most parks, this one truly comes alive at night. The undeveloped land and lakeshore creates an ideal space for looking into the heavens. Come for meteor showers, for a chance to spot the Northern Lights, or just everyday stargazing. No camping is offered at the site, which makes this truly a day (well, day-and-night) trip.

Hiawatha Water Trail

Multiple access points from Big Bay to Grand Marais
hiawathawatertrail.org

Kayaking on Lake Superior is becoming increasingly popular. A good sea kayak is capable of plying the waves with safety and speed and can get into the lake's hidden coves and bays easier than a canoe. One popular route is the Hiawatha Water Trail, where you can expect to see lighthouses, shipwrecks, and some of the most beautiful rock formations on the lake. This trail of more than 120 miles extends from Big Bay to Grand Marais and traverses the Pictured Rocks National Lakeshore. There are multiple access points along the trail, as well as a number of campgrounds.

Huron River Water Trail

Multiple access points from Commerce Township to South Rockwood;
see website below for an interactive trail map
huronriverwatertrail.org

The Huron River flows into Lake Erie, and for 104 miles it connects communities such as Milford, Dexter, Ann Arbor, Ypsilanti, and Flat Rock. It can take five days to paddle the full distance, but an online trip planner can help you select a shorter route. With a usually gentle current, the river is worth checking out, but it does have some rocky rapids, so be sure the section you choose to float matches your ability. For those who would prefer something other than canoeing, the river is good for swimming and catch-and-release fishing. Guided tours are also available. *Note:* The Huron Water Trail passes through several state recreation areas; launching in any of these requires a Michigan Recreation Passport (see page 5 for more information).

Huron Sunrise Trail

Rogers City to 40 Mile Point Lighthouse
trailscouncil.org/huron-sunrise-trail-2

The 10-mile long Huron Sunrise Trail is the perfect way to discover the beauty of Lake Huron, a Great Lake that gets less recognition and publicity than its more famous neighbors, Michigan and Superior. The paved trail makes for a nice walk or bike ride and is a great way to explore the dunes, beaches, streams, parks, forests, and other natural beauties of Lake Huron's shoreline. A spur trail leads into the Herman Vogler Conservation Area, which features additional hiking and mountain biking options.

13 Isle Royale National Park

Houghton Visitor Center 800 E. Lakeshore Drive, Houghton 49931-1896; (906) 482-0984
For directions to the island, see nps.gov/isro/planyourvisit/directions.htm

This is one of the least-visited national parks, but that's only because it's one of the most remote, consisting almost entirely of wilderness. If you love rustic hiking or backpacking, this is the place to be. Like Lake Superior, which surrounds it, the park is rugged, challenging, and rewarding. Hikers can choose loops on either end of the 45-mile long island or walk from end to end. If you're lucky, you may glimpse a moose or a wolf; wolf–moose interactions have been studied on this island since 1958. To reach the island, you need to take a ferry or a plane. There is a lodge at Rock Harbor, along with a visitor center and a dock store. The Windigo area, on the island's southwest end, has a campground, a visitor center complex, a store, and two rustic rental cabins. Boats leave from Houghton and Copper Harbor in Michigan, and seaplanes fly out of nearby Hancock. On the Minnesota side of the lake, ferry transportation is available from Grand Portage, and seaplane flights leave from Grand Marais. The island is open to visitors from April 16 to October 31, but the Houghton Visitor Center, on the mainland, is open year-round.

14 Jordan River

Warner Township to Lake Charlevoix in East Jordan
tinyurl.com/jordanrivermi

The 33-mile Jordan River was the first stream designated in the Michigan Natural Rivers Program. From rapids to long lulls, the river offers a variety of conditions and should entertain all paddlers. If you don't have a boat, nearby outfitters are available, and they can also let you know about river conditions and provide shuttle service. By the way, the river is a "world-class" brook trout stream, so bring your fishing gear and don't be in too much of a hurry to reach the river's end.

15 Kal-Haven Trail

Eastern trailhead 4143 10th St. N., Kalamazoo 49009

Western trailhead: just east of Bailey Avenue (less than 0.1 mile north of Bailey and East Wells Street), South Haven 49090
kalhaven.org, traillink.com/trail/kal-haven-trail-sesquicentennial-state-park

This trail, which follows the route of the former Kalamazoo and South Haven Railroad, is 34.5 miles long and covers the distance from Kalamazoo to South Haven. Reminders of the trail's past as a railway line can be found in the form of old depot stations and a caboose that now serve as visitor centers and museums. The crushed-limestone surface that covers much of the trails works fine for road bikes and mountain bikes alike and makes a wonderful hiking path, since it has more give than asphalt. Horses are allowed on 11 miles of the trail, and cross-country skiers use it in the winter. If you're looking for a longer ride, consider combining this trail with the nearby Kalamazoo Trail.

Lakeshore Trail

Southern trailhead Ottawa Beach Road just east of Holland State Park beach parking, Holland 49424

Northern trailhead Grand Haven State Park, 14035 Lakeshore Ave., Grand Haven 49417
mitrails.org/lakeshore-trail.php

Sand dunes, a tunnel of trees, and blue water say it all. This is an inspiring ride, and lake breezes make for a cool ride, even in the middle of summer. Paralleling the Lake Michigan shoreline, this trail connects Grand Haven and Holland State Parks (*note:* Michigan Recreation Passport required in both parks; see page 5), and several other parks provide good access and rest points along the route, including Kirk Park, Tunnel Park, and Rosy Mound Natural Area. Each offers a place to rest, picnic, play, and explore. On a hot day, you also can take a dip in the lake to cool off.

Lansing River Trail

Multiple trailheads in Lansing and East Lansing
lansingrivertrail.org/map

A mix of wooden boardwalks and asphalt trail, this is a classic ride along the Red Cedar and Grand Rivers. With a blend of urban and natural scenery, this ride is very popular and riders should be content to stick to a leisurely pace, as this trail can be busy. With possible stops at Potter Park Zoo, the Brenke Fish Ladder, the R. E. Olds Transportation Museum (see page 75), Impression 5 Science Center (see page 158), and the historic Turner Dodge House, there is no limit to how much time you can spend here. The Michigan Capitol Building and downtown area are additional areas you can explore.

22 Various locations

18 Leelanau Trail

Southern trailhead East Carter Road (about 1 mile north of Traverse City), Greilickville 49684

Northern trailhead North Dumas Road (just west of North West Bay Shore Drive), Suttons Bay 49682
traversetrails.org/trail/leelanau-trail

On the 17-mile Leelanau Trail, you can bike or hike past farms and orchards, as well as through beautiful hardwood forests. In the spring, enjoy the blossoms in the forests and orchards, and in the summer relax amid the shade. Stop by the historic Potato Barn for some history or visit the nearby Leo Creek Preserve to learn about permaculture and Michigan's outdoors. Be sure to return in all seasons, as the autumn leaves are quite a sight and the trail is groomed for skiing in the winter.

19 Mackinac Island Biking

M-185 (Lake Shore Boulevard), Mackinac Island
mackinacisland.org/see/explore-by-bike

This is the only bike trail in the state that is actually a road, and it's a road that doesn't allow cars. You read that right: M-185 doesn't allow cars. It's just you, your bike, and the horses. The road spans 8.2 miles and encircles the island, leading to rest stops, historic points, and great vistas. You might have to ride it twice, once to look inland and the other to look out to the beautiful waters of Lake Huron. Even though the road isn't particularly long, it's recommended that you allow 1–3 hours for the circuit. For a fee, the ferry to the island will transport your bike, or you can just rent bikes on the island. (Also see the profile in "Island Destinations," page 126.)

20 Manistee River

Hodenpyl Dam Pond near Mesick to Lake Michigan in Manistee
tinyurl.com/manisteeriver, visitmanisteecounty.com/project/big-manistee-river

The Manistee River is a good river for novice paddlers, particularly the lower portion. (A 15-mile section from Tippy Dam Pond in Brethren to the Rainbow Bend access in Manistee is designated as a National Recreation River; another 8.8 miles of adjacent land along the river's eastern shore, from Tippy Dam Pond to Hodenpyl Dam Pond, is designated as the Manistee River Trail.) There are also spots well suited to fishing and tubing. If you're quiet, you may see a variety of animals, including mink, deer, bears, otters, muskrats, and beavers. Mornings and evenings are the best times to spot wildlife. Eagles, ospreys, and herons are common sights, and songbirds love the island and shoreline thickets. Other sights include the dams and the Little Mac Suspension Bridge.

21 Marquette City Multi-Use Path

Southern trailhead Bayou Street at US 41, Harvey 49855

Northern trailhead Presque Isle Park, Peter White Drive, Marquette 49855
mitrails.org/marquette-city-multi-use-path.php

Marquette's harbor is home to an active marina, a lighthouse, and a maritime museum. The two iron ore docks on Lake Superior—one of which is still in operation—are like monuments in the water and call to mind the city's historical relationship with iron mining. The city of Marquette itself has historic brick buildings and Victorian mansions and is home to Northern Michigan University. Presque Isle Park, a forested peninsula on the northeast side of the city, is a popular spot for nature lovers and families alike. The best thing for hikers and bikers is that all of these wonderful landmarks are connected by a 17-mile network of paved trails. With so much to see and Lake Superior to keep you cool while you explore, you can't go wrong.

2 North Country National Scenic Trail

Passes through North Dakota, Minnesota, Wisconsin, Michigan, Ohio, Pennsylvania, New York, and Vermont
northcountrytrail.org

How about a little 4,600-mile hike? That just might exceed a day trip, so how about sampling Michigan's portion of this magnificent national trail? Michigan can lay claim to nearly a quarter of the trail, and this vast distance means there are many different hiking options for all different skill levels and interests. The trail goes through state forests, state parks, national parks, refuges and other public lands, providing ways to discover Michigan by "connecting the dots." Dedicated hikers can participate in the Hike 100 Challenge, which asks hikers to complete 100 minutes of hiking on the trail. Information about the challenge, as well as maps and other planning resources, is available at the website.

23 Paint Creek Trail

Southern trailhead 400 Sixth St., Rochester 48307

Northern trailhead 383 S. Broadway St., Lake Orion 48362
paintcreektrail.org

In 1983, this section of the Michigan Central and Penn Central railway lines was converted to the Paint Creek Trail. According to the Rails-to-Trails Conservancy, this was the first rail-trail in the state, making it a historic ride. But the history is not as important as the ride itself, and its forests, fields, wetlands, and its namesake, Paint Creek can be a welcome surprise to those not from the Greater Detroit area. Only 8.9 miles long, the ride stretches between Rochester and Lake Orion and makes for an easy there-and-back jaunt, eliminating the need for a shuttle. The limestone surface is 8 feet wide and is open for nonmotorized use year-round. This popular trail was named a National Recreation Trail in 2006.

24 Pere Marquette National Scenic River

Baldwin to Pere Marquette Lake in Ludington
visitpmriver.com

Michigan is home to many firsts, but this site is a really significant one for river lovers. The Pere Marquette River was the first waterway in Michigan to be designated a National Wild and Scenic River. Spring fed, the river begins near Baldwin and is the longest free-flowing river system in the Lower Peninsula. The river is a favorite for boaters, paddlers, and fishers alike, and its rocky shores, pools, and broad marshlands make it an engaging trip however you choose to enjoy it. The 66 miles designated as a Wild and Scenic River stretch from the river branch junction near Baldwin downstream to the Old Highway 31 Bridge in Scottville. *Note:* Unlike the shorelines o many other Michigan rivers, most of the Pere Marquette's shoreline is privately owned, so please be respectful of property owners, and be sure to use only public access points.

25 Pere Marquette State Trail & Pere Marquette Rail Trail

Pere Marquette State Trail Maple Street in Clare to Michigan Avenue in Baldwin

Pere Marquette Rail Trail East Fourth Street/Pine Street in Clare to Chippewa Trail near Ashman Street/Ann Street in Midland
traillink.com/trail/pere-marquette-state-trail, peremarquetterailtrail.org

You can access the two Pere Marquette trails from Clare, with the Pere Marquette State Trail heading west and the Pere Marquette Rail Trail heading east. The western trail is 53 miles of paved and crushed limestone surfaces and ends in Baldwin, while the eastern trail runs 30 miles to Midland. Both trails, which are connected by a 1.5-mile on-road ride, feature all the scenery mid-Michigan has to offer. Be sure to visit the Pere Marquette State Trail Welcome Center in Reed City. On the Pere Marquette Rail Trail, a must-see is the Tridge—a structure consisting of three bridges that all connect in the middle.

6 Pictured Rocks National Lakeshore

Munising Falls Visitor Center (open year-round) 1505 Sand Point Road, Munising 49862; (906) 387-3700

Grand Sable Visitor Center (open summer only) E21090 County Road H-58, Seney; (906) 494-2660
nps.gov/piro

Pictured Rocks National Lakeshore is an adventurer's paradise, known for its spectacular cliffs, vistas, and dunes. There are many ways to enjoy the lakeshore. Boat tours give an unparalleled view of the area, including the titular Pictured Rocks, but you'll find many other things to see and do as well. The trails are well maintained and lead hikers to hidden streams and waterfalls, overlooks, beaches, and even views of shipwrecks. If you can spare the time, a short backpacking trip is the perfect way to enjoy the scenery. Traveling with little ones? Don't worry; there are numerous activities for kids and families, too!

Pontiac Lake Recreation Area

7800 Gale Road, Waterford 48327; (248) 666-1020
tinyurl.com/pontiaclake

Just minutes from Pontiac and covering nearly 3,800 acres, this recreation area is the perfect place to escape the city and provides opportunities for visitors of all types. There are many adventures to be had here, and there are activities to partake in during each season. Bird-watching, horseback riding, biking, and hiking are perennial favorites, as is simple relaxation. Many evenings, you can also find local enthusiasts flying miniature model airplanes at one of the park's fields. *Note:* Michigan Recreation Passport required (see page 5).

28 Porcupine Mountains Wilderness State Park

33303 Headquarters Road, Ontonagon 49953; (906) 885-5275
tinyurl.com/porcupinemtnsstatepark

Home to 90 miles of backcountry trails and 35,000 acres of virgin forest, there are numerous hiking options in this state park. Lake of the Clouds is the most popular destination in the park; set in a deep cleft in the mountain ridges, it's as close to the Scottish Highlands as you can get in the United States.

Keep in mind that this is a wilderness park and even a day trip calls for a more rugged hike. The Lake Superior Trail has many fantastic views of the nearby lake, but the trail is 17 miles long and rugged. Pace yourself, or better yet, consider reserving one of their back-country camping sites and make this more than a simple day trip. *Note:* Michigan Recreation Passport required (see page 5).

Sunset at Sleeping Bear Dunes National Lakeshore

29 Sleeping Bear Dunes National Lakeshore

Philip A. Hart Visitor Center 9922 W. Front St., Empire 49630;
(231) 326-4700, ext. 5010
nps.gov/slbe

The Lake Michigan shoreline is famous for its dunes, and rightfully so, but the Sleeping Bear Dunes area is truly something special. (The lakeshore gets its name from an Anishinabe legend about a mother bear, Mishe Mokwa, who fled what is now Wisconsin with her cubs after fires destroyed their forest home.) Geologically, these are perched dunes—sand atop an old glacial ridge. Because of that ridge, these dunes are unusually tall, reaching as high as 400 feet. There are many ways to appreciate and have fun on the dunes; hiking, dune climbing, and rolling are all options, as are sea kayaking and simple relaxation. If you love hiking, don't forget to go inland and follow the trails to bogs, lakes, and forested glens.

0 Waterloo Recreation Area

16345 McClure Road, Chelsea 48118; (734) 475-8307
tinyurl.com/waterloorecreationarea, thebig400.com

This is the largest state park in the Lower Peninsula, and its landscape is quite different from that in the U.P. Part of The Big 400, an initiative to balance "nature and commerce" in the Chelsea area, this park is home to 11 inland lakes and 47 miles of hiking trails. Not surprisingly, boating, swimming, and fishing are all popular pursuits, but so are horseback riding, hiking, and, in the winter, cross-country skiing. The ski trails are ungroomed, however, and skiing can require intermediate-to-expert skills. *Note:* Michigan Recreation Passport required (see page 5).

Yankee Springs Recreation Area

2104 S. Briggs Road, Middleville 49333; (269) 795-9081
tinyurl.com/yankeesprings

This 5,200-acre recreation area is home to nine lakes that are replete with camping and fishing options, but don't miss the area's many trails, its wildflowers, and bird-watching opportunities, especially during migration season. In winter, the fun doesn't stop, as Yankee Springs offers cross-country skiing trails, ice fishing opportunities, and more. *Note:* Michigan Recreation Passport required (see page 5).

Seney Trumpeter Swans

THE GREAT LAKES PROVIDE a thriving range of habitats for local fauna. From forests to lakeshore to marshes, there are a variety of places where you can go to see native species. Migrating birds can be seen in large numbers in the spring and fall as they use the limited passageways across the lakes. For lovers of nonwinged creatures, there are fish hatcheries, wildlife refuges, and game areas. Or see more-exotic creatures at the American Zoological Association–accredited zoos in the state.

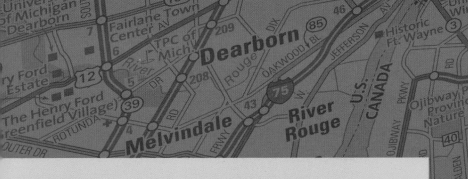

FOR BIRD-WATCHERS & ANIMAL LOVERS

(continued on next page)

Once endangered and always beloved, the Kirtland's Warbler nests in only a few places, including Michigan

1 Bernard W. Baker Sanctuary

21145 15 Mile Road, Bellevue 49021; (517) 580-7364
michiganaudubon.org/our-conservation-impact/bird-sanctuaries

Cranes are revered worldwide, but they are also endangered throughout much of their range. That is no longer true for the sandhill crane, thanks to groups such as the Michigan Audubon Society, which created this sanctuary in 1941. Home to a variety of habitats, there can be as many as 5,000 cranes here at one time, as well as a variety of other birds, including ospreys, eagles, waterfowl, hawks, and marsh birds. With patience (and a good pair of binoculars), you can see many of these species when bird-watching. The October CraneFest, in the adjacent Kiwanis Youth Area, is an excellent event to add to a day at the sanctuary.

2 Binder Park Zoo

7400 Division Drive, Battle Creek 49014; (269) 979-1351
binderparkzoo.org

Not all zoos boast vast acreages or a wide variety of species. Binder Park Zoo, however, has both. With 433 acres of forest and wetland, the zoo offers approximately 140 unique species. The zoo is home to one of the largest giraffe herds in America, and hand-feeding the giraffes is the highlight for most visitors. The zoo also features a free tram ride and a farm with domestic animals, but its true purpose is to provide learning opportunities and promote species survival.

3 Detroit River International Wildlife Refuge

Large Lakes Research Station 9311 Groh Road, Grosse Ile 48138; (734) 365-021
fws.gov/refuge/detroit_river

The first wildlife refuges were established under President Theodore Roosevelt due to the growing threats that unchecked hunting and commerce posed to wildlife. Today, there are more than 540 refuges and this one holds the distinction of being the first International Wildlife Refuge in North America. With more than 6,000 acres of marshland on the lower Detroit River and the shore of Lake Erie, this refuge provides numerous recreation and education activities.

Humbug Marsh is the centerpiece of the refuge, which also contains the last mile of natural shoreline along the U.S. portion of the Detroit River.

4 Detroit Zoo and Belle Isle Nature Center

Zoo 8450 W. 10 Mile Road, Royal Oak 48067; (248) 541-5717
detroitzoo.org

Belle Isle Nature Center 176 Lakeside Drive, Detroit 48207; (313) 852-4056
belleislenaturecenter.detroitzoo.org

With exhibits focusing on Australia, Africa, Asia, the Arctic and Antarctic, plus Amphibiville (a national amphibian conservation center), the Detroit Zoo is on the A list. This zoo is home to aardvarks, zebras, and hundreds of species in between. Highlights include the Giraffe Encounter, where you can feed the zoo's tallest creatures, and the lion habitat, where you can get face to face with the big cats. If you're lucky, you'll encounter some of the free-roaming wildlife in addition to the captive species in this clean, well-run zoo. The Detroit Zoo also operates the Belle Isle Nature Center, a smaller display of animals native to Michigan. A third nature experience run by the Detroit Zoo, the Great Lakes Center for Nature, will soon be opening in Macomb County; check the zoo's website for updates.

Kirtland's Warbler Tours

Tours offered in May and June at two locations:

Huron National Forest, Mio Ranger District 107 McKinley Road, Mio 48647; (989) 826-3252, ext. 3334

Hartwick Pines State Park Visitor Center 4216 Ranger Road, Grayling 49738; (989) 348-2537; Michigan Audubon, (517) 580-7364
fws.gov/midwest/eastlansing/te/kiwa/tour.html, tinyurl.com/usfswarblertour, michiganaudubon.org/kirtlands-warbler-tours

Sometimes just a bit of birdsong coming through an open car window is enough to signal that you're about to observe one of the rarest warblers in the world. In 1987, there were only 167 male Kirtland's warblers living in the jack pine forest, and they represented the worldwide population. Then, ornithologists and foresters joined forces and took action. Because of these human allies, this bluish-gray-and-yellow warbler is now a success story that you can see for yourself. There are two options for these guided tours: one that leaves from Hartwick Pines State Park in Grayling with the Michigan Audubon Society and one in Huron National Forest with the U.S. Forest Service. (*Note:* The USFS tour has been canceled for 2021; instead, a self-guided driving itinerary is available at tinyurl.com/usfswarblertour (see links under "Self-Guided Jack Pine Wildlife Viewing Tour"). A Michigan Recreation Passport is required to enter Hartwick Pines State Park; see page 5.)

8 Various locations

6 Lake Bluff Bird Sanctuary

2890 Lakeshore Road, Manistee 49660; (231) 723-4042
michiganaudubon.org/lake-bluff-bird-sanctuary

Michigan Audubon strives to connect birds and people for the benefit of both through efforts in research, education and conservation. It has done just that at the Lake Bluff Bird Sanctuary. The sanctuary, which was originally designed to be an arboretum, occupies more than 1,500 feet of Lake Michigan shoreline and more than 2 miles of preserved and maintained trails on its 76 acres. Many notable specimens of trees have been preserved here, such as a California redwood, a ginkgo, a giant sequoia, a sycamore, and many large cottonwoods. Also notable are the 170-plus bird species, which both nest and migrate through the area. Keep your eyes open for bald eagles, rare and common shorebirds, and migrating warblers. This sanctuary is the result of a gift from a Michigan family and is now home to a quaint bed-and-breakfast.

7 Leslie Science & Nature Center

1831 Traver Road, Ann Arbor 48105; (734) 997-1553
lesliesnc.org

Upon their deaths in 1976, Eugene and Emily Leslie donated their 200-plus acres of land to the City of Ann Arbor. They wanted to preserve natural habitat amid a developing city, and today, their land is home to the Leslie Science & Nature Center. The Center continues to promote the goals of the Leslies and strives to be a place for promoting open nature, family experiences, and education. Highlights of the Science & Nature Center include the Critter House and the Birds of Prey and Raptor Enclosures. The magnificent birds of prey on-site are all victims of extreme injury, which makes them unfit for return to life in the wild.

8 Michigan's Birding Trails

Various locations throughout Michigan

Beaver Island beaverislandbirdingtrail.org

Michigan Audubon michiganaudubon.org/go-birding/birding-trails

Saginaw Bay saginawbaybirding.org

Sleeping Bear sleepingbearbirdingtrail.org

Sunrise Coast tinyurl.com/sunrisecoastbirdingtrail

Superior superiorbirdingtrail.com

These assorted travel routes connect you with excellent birding hot spots, and they are a great way to explore the state and to look for outstanding birds at the same time. From Au Sable to Saginaw Bay, these trails allow you to mix nature and travel. You can also visit local towns along the way and learn about the various parks, the birds, and their habitats. Each trail offers something new; many can be explored in conjunction with birding festivals, or they can just be added on to existing vacation plans. Contact each site for maps and bird lists, then enjoy the adventure!

Millie Hill Trail and the Millie Mine Bat Cave

Mine Shaft Park Avenue off East A Street, Iron Mountain 49801; (800) 236-2447
info@ironmountain.org

We know—bats aren't the most popular animals. But ask a person in the middle of mosquito season if they'd like something to prey upon those lovely little bloodsuckers, and the bat may suddenly become more popular. But who would think that you could come to an abandoned mine shaft in Michigan's Upper Peninsula and find one of the largest bat colonies in North America. Up to a million bats were once found here; unfortunately, White Nose Syndrome, a fungal disease that kills bats, has since ravaged the area's bat population. The best times to view the remaining bats are when they emerge from hibernation in April and May, and when they prepare for winter in September and October. Signage providing information on Michigan's mining history and the important role bats play in the environment is present at the mine site and along the Millie Hill Trail.

Oden State Fish Hatchery

Hatchery 8258 S. Ayr Road, Alanson 49764; (231) 347-4689, ext. 12

Visitor Center 3377 US 31, Oden, 49764; (231) 348-0998
tinyurl.com/odenstatefishhatchery

Whether it takes place in streams, in small inland lakes, or in the Great Lakes, fishing is popular throughout Michigan, and the state fish hatcheries are kept busy supporting this highly popular form of recreation. Fortunately, some have chosen to share the hatchery experience with visitors. Visitors at the Oden State Fish Hatchery are treated to a variety of attractions: hiking trails, an underwater viewing chamber, signs for self-guided experiences, and even fish ponds where you can feed the lunkers. Especially noteworthy is seeing the train car that once

transported fish from the hatchery to the lakes—imagine the fish stories the fish got from that! Seeing the fish swirling below your feet in their ponds may not be the same as feeling them on the line, but it's breathtaking all the same.

11 Otis Farm Bird Sanctuary

3560 Havens Road, Hastings 49058; (517) 580-7364
michiganaudubon.org/faq-items/otis-farm-bird-sanctuary

A Michigan Audubon sanctuary that encompasses 128 acres in rural Barry County, this site butts up against a Globally Important Bird Area for the public to explore. Avid bird-watchers will want to keep an eye open for sightings of Henslow's sparrow and the cerulean warbler, but the property and surrounding area are biologically diverse and home to many bird species. In June a special Cerulean Watch Weekend honors of the small bird whose population numbers have fallen drastically in the last half a century.

12 Pointe Mouillee State Game Area

37205 Mouillee Road (US 2), Rockwood 48173; (734) 379-9692
tinyurl.com/pointemouilleesga, ptemouilleewaterfowlfestival.org

When it comes to ducks, some fans of these birds bring along binoculars, while others bring hunting gear. Whatever their equipment, both groups love waterfowl. At Pointe Mouillee—one of the largest freshwater marsh restoration projects in North America—the Huron River enters Lake Erie, and during migration, its more than 4,000 acres of restored marshland serve as a temporary home to thousands of waterfowl, shorebirds, wading birds, and birds of prey. Late summer and early fall are the peak times for the magnificent concentration. In September there is a Waterfowl Festival that can help you get the most out of your visit.

3 Potter Park Zoo

1301 S. Pennsylvania Ave., Lansing 48912; (517) 483-4222
potterparkzoo.org

Located along the river corridor and biking and walking trails, the Potter Park Zoo is not far from the state capitol. Though not large, the 20-acre zoo is big enough for an excellent experience. The zoo features some rare animals, such as Amur tigers and a snow leopard; this is a far cry from the park's early days back in 1920, when a group of elk were moved to the park and became the first zoo residents. Now the zoo boasts over 110 species, including a rare and healthy black rhino calf born in 2019. Speaking of little ones, if you bring children with you, the Farmyard EdVentures area is a good choice, as is the Wings of Wonder exhibit, where you can feed the birds.

4 Seney National Wildlife Refuge

1674 Refuge Entrance Road, Seney 49883; (906) 586-9851
fws.gov/refuge/seney

This is one of the great wildlife refuges. When you visit, you'll be greeted by swans, scolded by geese, and have a chance to see a wide variety of other wildlife. The wetlands and forests in this area were once known as the Great Manistique Swamp and, like many wetlands and forests of the Midwest, they have a history of being significantly altered by humans. Despite the alterations, the refuge has a rich mosaic of habitats and ecosystems, managed for an array of ecological conditions that benefit a variety of wildlife such as beavers, ducks, loons, turtles, otters, bears, sandhill cranes, wolves, snowshoe hares, and warblers. Many of these species can be spotted along the 7-mile-long Marshland Wildlife Drive; the more adventurous may want to consider bicycling the back roads, hiking the ski trails, or paddling the Manistique River. Before venturing out onto the refuge, check out the visitor center, open daily mid-May through mid-October, for more information and tips on what to look for.

Shiawassee National Wildlife Refuge

6975 Mower Road, Saginaw 48601; (989) 777-5930
fws.gov/refuge/shiawassee

The American Bird Conservancy has designated this refuge as an Important Bird Area because of the significant number of migratory geese, ducks, shorebirds, and songbirds that pass through each year. The refuge was founded in 1953, primarily as a habitat for migrating Canada geese. You can view more than 270 species of birds and various other wildlife species on the refuge's trails or the Wildlife Drive along the Shiawassee River.

16 Tawas Point Birding Festival

Tawas Point State Park 686 Tawas Beach Road, East Tawas 48730, (989) 362-5041; Michigan Audubon, (517) 580-7364
michiganaudubon.org/news-events/signature-events/tawas-bird-fest

Become a birder! It doesn't matter if you've been filling your bird feeders for a lifetime or if you're just now deciding to see what birding is all about: this birding festival in Tawas Point State Park is a wonderful place to begin. Here you can catch workshops, go on field trips with experienced and enthusiastic people, and learn about birding. With the scenery of Tuttle Marsh, Clark's Marsh, and Tawas Point State Park and its classic lighthouse, you will not only be observing birds but also enjoying beautiful landscapes. The festival takes place in May, when warblers are likely to add color and motion to the event. Keep your binoculars handy; more than 170 species have been recorded here! (*Note:* Canceled for 2021 but expected to return in 2022; check with Michigan Audubon for the latest information. A Michigan Recreation Passport is required to enter Tawas Poin State Park; see page 5 for more information.)

17 Tuttle Marsh Wildlife Area

Huron-Manistee National Forests Old US 23 at Tuttle Marsh Road, Oscoda 48750; (989) 739-0728
n-sport.com/tuttlemarshwildlifearea.html

Wetlands were once drained in an effort to eliminate them from rural lands, but today we realize how diverse and species-intense these places can be. Today, ditches and water controls are used to maintain water quality, and this has resulted is an enrichment of the groundwater, and a paradise for waterfowl, mammals, and amphibians. A drive through this 5,000-acre wildlife area will allow you to observe osprey nests, sandhill cranes, a great blue heron rookery, and shorebirds on the mudflats. Waterfowl such as rails and bitterns can be abundant and elusive birds and hide in the vegetation, so you can only hear their calls. If you're lucky, maybe you'll catch a quick, satisfying glance of a black bear, a beaver, or a bobcat.

8 Whitefish Point Bird Observatory

Visitor Center 18330 N. Whitefish Point Road, Paradise 49768; (517) 580-7364
wpbo.org

Whitefish Point is the third-largest peninsula on Lake Superior's south shore and the shortest distance across the lake to Canada, at 19 miles. Because of this geography, Whitefish Point sees a large concentration of hawks, falcons, eagles, and owls during spring migration. An average of 20,000 raptors fly through the area as Whitefish Point Bird Observatory (WPBO) continues its 40-plus years of migration research. The Spring Fling, held during the last weekend in April, is WPBO's annual migration celebration and the official opening of the Owl's Roost interpretive center and gift shop. In the summer, the Point becomes home to the endangered piping plover. These shorebirds nest along the sandy cobblestone beach. Another summer visitor is the juvenile northern saw-whet owl. Recently hatched, these owls pass through in the hundreds in July and August. During the spring, summer, and fall, WPBO conducts nightly owl banding for these and the eight other species of owls that can be found. Autumn brings our largest concentration of waterfowl and shorebirds here. A seasonal average of 80,000 waterbirds, loons, grebes, ducks, mergansers, and geese follow the Lake Superior shoreline on their way to the Gulf Coast or Atlantic coastline. The fall also brings an end to another year of migration data collection. Because of this phenomenal flyway, WPBO is designated a Globally Important Bird Area by the American Bird Conservancy. Whitefish Point is truly a birding paradise.

W. K. Kellogg Biological Station

3700 E. Gull Lake Drive, Hickory Corners 49060; (269) 671-5117
kbs.msu.edu

The primary purpose of the Kellogg Biological Station (KBS) is to perform ecological research, but don't let that stop you from making a day trip here. Affiliated with Michigan State University, KBS also works to educate the public, and everyone is welcome! Kellogg Forest, the trails, and the picnic areas are open until dusk, and there are self-guided tours available of the Kellogg Bird Sanctuary and the Kellogg Manor House. If you want to get a more behind-the-scenes experience, sign up for one of the guided tours. Be aware that the tours through the Kellogg Farm Pasture Dairy Center and the Long-Term Ecological Research areas are restricted to adults only.

The Detroit Institute of Arts

MAYBE IT'S THE INSPIRATION of the Great Lakes or the beauty of the wild inland forests, but Michigan is blessed with an abundance of art. Ranging from small-town museums and outdoor sculpture parks to major exhibits at more well-known museums, almost anywhere you turn in Michigan, you'll find the fine arts.

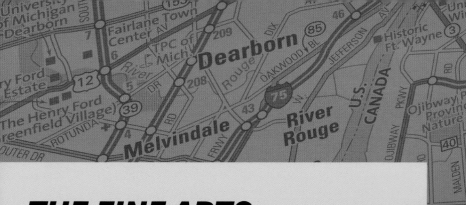

THE FINE ARTS

(continued on next page)

Scenery at the Frederik Meijer Gardens & Sculpture Park

1 AACTMAD (Ann Arbor Community for Traditional Music and Dance)

4531 Concourse Drive, Ann Arbor 48108; (872) 222-8623
aactmad.org

Dance is a part of almost every culture, and many ethnic groups and cultures have their own specific kinds of dances. Familiar examples include Morris dance, Celtic dance, and contra dance. Hosting over 100 events each year, this organization seeks to popularize traditional music and dance. Join them for lessons in a variety of English, American, and European dancing styles. You can also find them at larger events such as the Dancing in the Streets festival over Labor Day weekend or the Melt into Spring English Country Dance Ball in March. Most of the dances emphasize community and welcome beginners, with or without a partner. Generally, all dances are taught or walked through before the music starts. Prefer to make music rather than listen to it? Join the Pittsfield Open Band for one of their open gig sessions to practice your reels, jigs, and waltzes.

2 Ann Arbor Folk Festival

The Ark   316 S. Main St., Ann Arbor 48104; (734) 761-1800 (for calls 9 a.m.–5 p.m. Monday–Friday); (734) 761-1818 (for calls 6:30 a.m.–11 p.m. on concert evenings)

Hill Auditorium, University of Michigan   825 N. University Ave., Ann Arbor 4810
theark.org/folk-festival

The Ann Arbor Folk Festival, held during the last weekend in January, is a celebration of traditional roots, folk, and ethnic music that began in 1976. A fundraiser for The Ark, a local nonprofit music venue founded in 1965, the festival aims to preserve these musical genres and share them with new audiences and established listeners. The event's long history is a testament to the quality of the project and the people who run it. If you can't make the festival, which is held at the University of Michigan's Hill Auditorium but was virtual in 2021, find year-round programming at The Ark, a 400-seat venue with outstanding performances from new and established artists. Also available are workshops, shows, and educational programming

3 Broad Museum

547 E. Circle Drive, East Lansing 48824; (517) 884-4800
broadmuseum.msu.edu

Named in honor of Eli and Edythe Broad, Michigan State alumni whose donation to the arts made this museum possible, the art in this museum starts on the outside. The building that houses the museum was designed by award-winning architect Zaha Hadid, and it is rumored to contain no right angles. This sense of breaking away from the traditional permeates the museum, which also runs a community art lab across the street. The museum was also used as a filming location in the movie *Batman vs. Superman: Dawn of Justice.*

4 Detroit Institute of Arts

5200 Woodward Ave., Detroit 48202; (313) 833-7900
dia.org

At over 65,000 pieces, this art collection is exhaustive, so it's OK if you need a few day trips here to take it all in. Here you'll find art from famous and little-known artists alike; art from all corners of the world, and art from early civilizations up to modern day. Designed by Paul Cret, the museum building was referred to as the "temple of art" as soon as it opened, and that title is still appropriate. The museum boasts that its collection is "one of the top six in the United States"; to us, the top attraction was the Diego Rivera mural that dominates the walls in the center court. This huge mural is a reflection on the industry and working people of Detroit; it is massive and colorful, and it's worth taking a trip to Detroit just to stand in its midst.

5 East Lansing Art Festival

410 Abbot Road, East Lansing 48823; (517) 319-6804
elartfest.com

This festival, held in downtown East Lansing, is often listed as one of the top fine-art festivals in the nation—the process of selecting artists to showcase their work at this event is highly competitive. The free event (usually held in May) blends juried fine art and craft exhibits with live music, children's activities, and various food options. Also be sure to head across Grand River Avenue to visit the **Michigan State University Spring Arts & Crafts Show,** which is usually held the same weekend (see uabevents.com/annualartscrafts for more information).

6 Ella Sharp Museum

3225 Fourth St., Jackson 49203; (517) 787-2320
ellasharp.org

This small museum is located in Sharp Park, where both the park and the museum are named for Ella Sharp, a prominent Jackson resident who willed her land to the city. The park complex and museum features a unique combination of art and history. The centerpiece of the museum is the 19th-century farmhouse, but the museum is also home to several galleries, exhibits pertaining to Jackson's history, rotating exhibits, and eight historical outbuildings.

7 Frederik Meijer Gardens & Sculpture Park

1000 E. Beltline Ave. NE, Grand Rapids 49525; (616) 957-1580, (888) 957-1580
meijergardens.org

One day is just not enough to really see and enjoy all this park has to offer. You can rush through, but art isn't about rushing around in order to check items off a list. The highlight of this park is the interplay between nature and art—nature that is valued for its artistic contributions as much as the sculptures are. Whether it is the outside gardens, the indoor floral displays, or the natural wetlands and forest, the natural scenery makes this a full, rich experience. There is also a Children's Garden that combines art and play. If you're not sure you really like art, this sculpture park is the place to visit. There is so much to engage with, you might just find that art becomes an exciting part of your own experience.

8 Gilmore International Keyboard Festival

359 S. Kalamazoo Mall, Ste. 101, Kalamazoo 49007; (269) 342-1166
thegilmore.org/festival

Since 1989, this biennial piano festival, held in the spring, has brought the best keyboard artists to Kalamazoo. Created in honor of a local businessman, this nationally prominent festival spans three weeks and has contests and awards in classical, jazz, chamber, and other forms of music. The emphasis is on young and promising artists. There is a Rising Stars performance series, as well as a Piano

Masters Series, both of which offer public concerts. (*Note:* Call or check the website for the latest information.)

9 Grand Rapids Art Museum

101 Monroe Center St. NW, Grand Rapids 49503; (616) 831-1000
artmuseumgr.org

In Grand Rapids, one of the most prominent artistic statements is Alexander Calder's famous sculpture *La Grande Vitesse* in the downtown area. It was this sculpture that inspired the museum to develop a collection of Calder's works, from sculpture to painting. Calder's works are not the only ones on display, however, and in the hundred year history of the museum, it has acquired over 6,000 pieces of art spanning across millennia. The museum is also doing its part for sustainability as the first-ever LEED Gold–certified art museum. This means that this beautiful building is also energy efficient, dispelling the notion that environmentally sensitive design cannot be interesting and appealing. The art here is just as significant as the building, with masters like Dürer, Rembrandt, Homer, and Warhol.

0 Hiawatha Traditional Music Festival

Marquette Tourist Park 2145 Sugar Loaf Ave., Marquette 49855; (906) 226-8575
hiawathamusic.org/about-the-hiawatha-festival

An event with a history of more than three decades of performance and entertainment, the Hiawatha Music Co-Op supports a three-day July festival of traditional American acoustic music and traditional dance. Drawing an audience from throughout the U.P. and across the country, the festival features a variety of traditional musical styles, including Cajun and Celtic, as well as folk and blues. These performers are often world-class musicians, and if you are an artist or a fan, you might like the "meet the artist" sessions or the musical instruction that is part of the festival schedule. There's fun for the little ones as well, with activities for children and teens all through the weekend. (*Note:* Call or check online for the latest information.)

Interlochen Center for the Arts

4000 Highway M-137, Interlochen 49643; (231) 276-7200
interlochen.org

If you walk on campus during one of the Interlochen Center's open houses, the saying "there's music in the air" will be a reality. As you walk from studio to studio and hear the different forms of music being played by the students, you'll be inspired, and that's just one of the options for the visitor. In addition to the students, there are guest

artists, lecturers and exhibits that enrich the overall art experience. If you're in the area without time to stop, you can tune in to their performances on public radio.

12 Kalamazoo Institute of Arts

314 S. Park St., Kalamazoo 49007; (269) 349-7775
kiarts.org

Formed in 1924, the Kalamazoo Institute of Arts has long held the belief that art is not only to be enjoyed—it is to be made, too. While you will find traditional collections and exhibitions, what makes this institute unique is the way it embraces local art and artists—including local schoolchildren. Each June, KIA hosts the Kalamazoo Art Fair, at which local artists exhibit their creations, making for a fun start to summer. The museum also hosts an art school that ensures local art will have a promising future. Because its exhibits are temporary, there's always something new to see.

13 Krasl Art Center

707 Lake Blvd., St. Joseph 49085; (269) 983-0271
krasl.org

Every great museum has a trademark exhibit, something that sets it apart from other museums. For the Krasl Art Center that something special is its nationally renowned collection of contemporary sculpture. The museum, which has indoor and outdoor exhibits, also includes an art lab, which they describe as "a venue for all artists who are pushing the boundaries of medium and form." Admission to the art center is always free, though a donation is suggested. Try to schedule your visit when the Krasl Art Fair on the Bluff is being held; *Sunshine Artist* magazine named it one of the best art fairs in the nation.

14 Marshall M. Fredericks Sculpture Museum

7400 Bay Road, Saginaw 48710; (989) 964-7125
marshallfredericks.org

After visiting this museum, it becomes clear how prevalent the sculpture of Marshall M. Fredericks (1908–98) is throughout Michigan. Once you recognize his style, you'll soon notice it all over the place. The distinct style and clean, uncomplicated lines of his sculptures convey a story, and often bring a smile. This museum features more than 200 works created over 70 years by Fredericks, the Detroit sculptor who developed an international reputation. In this museum you can see how the art was created, comparing the different samples, and then walking around outdoors in the sculpture garden, where the pieces are truly at home. This museum and the sculpture garden are located within the campus of Saginaw Valley State University.

5 Michigan Legacy Art Park

7300 Mountainside Drive, Thompsonville 49683; (231) 378-4963
michlegacyartpark.org

The theme of this art park, located at Crystal Mountain is "Where Art, Nature, and History Meet." Complete with a wooded preserve, fresh air, hiking trails, and more than 40 sculptures that depict the history of Michigan, this is an inspiring place. In addition to the sculptures, there are 30 poetry stones along the pathways. To discover what is here, pick up a trail map at the trailhead. Take along a picnic, hike the trails and then talk about the history depicted around you; it might just give you a greater appreciation of the state. This park is open all year during daylight hours.

Michigan Legacy Art Park

19

2016-18

16 Motown Museum

2648 W. Grand Blvd., Detroit 48208; (313) 875-2264
motownmuseum.org

For anyone born in the rock and roll era, this museum is an icon of music and art. Motown Records started out as a small place that made big hits. Berry Gordy Jr. christened an obscure little house in Detroit "Hitsville, U.S.A.," and it resulted in some of the most memorable songs, artists, and performances in entertainment history. At the Motown Museum there are photographs and memorabilia that tell the story, but it's the music that will make the connection for you, and with artists like Smokey Robinson and the Miracles, Martha and the Vandellas, The Four Tops, The Jackson 5, and The Supremes, there are many connections to be made. And the most amazing fact is that the bands listed above are just a sampling of what Hitsville has produced.

17 Museum of Contemporary Art Detroit

4454 Woodward Ave., Detroit 48201; (313) 832-6622
mocadetroit.org

Bringing contemporary art to the art-loving public is a big task. Forms and formats change over time, and the general public is not always up to date when it comes to the newest art movements. So when you visit this museum, known to the locals as MOCAD, test your open-mindedness and explore the new forms without comparing them to the old. Even the gift-shop items here differ from those of traditional art museums. Let yourself be shocked, moved, and challenged.

18 Pewabic Pottery National Historic Landmark

10125 E. Jefferson Ave., Detroit 48214; (313) 626-2000
pewabic.org

Dating back to 1903, this National Historic Landmark has a long history, and to this day it continues to boast a tradition of craftmanship that is reflected in the works it produces. Pewabic Pottery vessels and tiles continue to be collector's items, and each is unique in color and design. Once you see the products, you will begin to recognize their creations in buildings around the state and in a variety of art collections. In addition, heirloom architectural items ordered from all over the world are made here. There are many ways to take part in the revival of an art form that has become rare: tour, shop, or take an education class at Pewabic and learn how to make your own pottery.

19 Saugatuck Center for the Arts

400 Culver St., Saugatuck 49453; (269) 857-2399
sc4a.org

The Saugatuck Center for the Arts offers year-round programming inside a renovated pie factory. This is a place for creativity, with classes, workshops, art exhibitions, a professional Equity summer theater, and performances featuring Grammy Award–winning performers. Music, theater, and film in an intimate 410-seat theater make this the place to be, and it attracts guests from around the country. The energy here is sure to inspire. As an art venue, what more could you want? While the building no longer features factory-produced pies, good food is still celebrated with a summer Green Market and other food-related events throughout the year.

20 University of Michigan Museum of Art

525 S. State St., Ann Arbor 48109-1354; (734) 764-0395
umma.umich.edu

Universities have played an important role in educating new artists and investing in the world of art. Following that tradition, this museum at the University of Michigan underwent a major expansion in 2009, which allowed the museum to triple its on-display collection of art. They like to think of their museum as a "cultural town square" and strive for it to be a leader and model in art museums at universities nationwide. With an art collection that dates back to the 1850s and access to the expansive world of contemporary art, this a perfect blend of old and new.

Lake Superior

BEACHES MIGHT MAKE YOU THINK of the Caribbean or of the Florida or California coasts, but those places have nothing on Michigan. Surrounded by Lakes Michigan, Superior, Huron, and Erie, and with more than 11,000 inland lakes and myriad rivers and streams, Michigan has more freshwater shoreline than any other state in the country. If that does not motivate you to put on your swimsuit, grab the sunscreen, and head for the beach, then it must be winter. (*Note:* A Michigan Recreation Passport is required at the state parks profiled in this section. See page 5 for more information.)

BEACHES & DUNES

(continued on next page)

ctured Rocks National Lakeshore

1 Aloha State Park

4347 Third St., Cheboygan 49721; (231) 625-2522
tinyurl.com/alohastatepark

This park isn't Hawaii—but in the summer, who needs it to be? Located on Mullett Lake, Aloha State Park campsites, a boat launch, and trails, and the park is only a short distance from the Straits of Mackinac and Lake Huron. The lake is perfect for swimming; it has a sandy bottom and features a nice gradual slope leading to deep water. Let's put it this way—Aloha State Park is a summer destination. A word of warning: if you want to camp here, it's so popular that you must reserve a site at least six months in advance.

2 Gillette Sand Dune Visitor Center

6585 Lake Harbor Road, Muskegon 49441; (231) 798-3573
facebook.com/gillettenatureassociation
tinyurl.com/gillettesanddunevisitorcenter

Located in P. J. Hoffmaster State Park, this center helps visitors understand sand dunes, which are as complex as they are beautiful. The center is centered atop a large sand dune, a perfect place to observe and appreciate the dunes on Lake Michigan's eastern shore. The center's excellent exhibits help visitors learn about dune ecology and just how fragile dunes really are—despite how strong and stable they may seem. The exhibits include dioramas, animations about dune formation, and many learning stations. Take the nearby Lake Michigan Trail to get a stunning look at the dunes and lake.

3 Holland State Park

2215 Ottawa Beach Road, Holland 49424; (616) 399-9390
tinyurl.com/hollandstatepark

This is not the place to find tulips, but the sunsets here are just as colorful and a perfect complement to Lake Michigan to the west. Lake Michigan isn't the only lake you'll find here, however; the park also includes Lake Macatawa and its beach. Sailboats often dot the blue water of Lake Michigan and add to the picturesque setting, but the beach is still the main attraction. Even if the weather changes, there' much to do, thanks to the two campgrounds, a picnic shelter, a new playground, and even a rustic lodge. We highly recommend the dune boardwalk. Because it is highly elevated, the boardwalk makes it easy to observe the lake, the dunes, and the well-known Big Red Lighthouse.

Ludington State Park

8800 W. M-116, Ludington 49431; (231) 843-2423
tinyurl.com/ludingtonstatepark, visitludington.com/statepark

Boasting a picturesque beachfront (as well as many popular regional and local beaches), this park is also home to some special features. If the waters of Lake Michigan are too rough or cold, you can swim at Hamlin Lake Beach, explore the 4-mile canoe trail, or visit Big Sable Point Lighthouse. If it's hiking you're interested in, there are 21 miles of trails through forests and across the sand dunes. This is also a park that lends itself well to photography, so bring your camera. The beach is perfect for beach volleyball, and there is plenty of room for your best sand castle. If this is a family event, you should find more than enough to do to satisfy everyone—from the beach bum to the angler.

Oval Beach

Oval Drive, Saugatuck 49453
Saugatuck-Douglas Visitors Bureau, 2902 Blue Star Highway, Douglas 49406;
(269) 857-1701
saugatuckcity.com/index.php/parks-recreation/oval-beach

Oval Beach was named one of the top 25 shorelines by Condé Nast's *Traveler Magazine,* and MTV ranked it even higher as one of the country's top five beaches. *National Geographic Traveler* named it one of the top two freshwater beaches in the United States and the *Chicago Tribune* ranked it the number-one beach on Lake Michigan. After endorsements like that, what can you do but see it for yourself? The beach has a lot going for it: its soft sand is vaunted and it's easy to access, plus the convenient concession stands make it easy to grab a snack. Others love the sunsets—where on the Lake Michigan coast is there *not* a great sunset? Keep in mind that given this beach's popularity, you may have a difficult time finding parking, though public transport is provided from any place in town. If you're looking for something a little less busy, all you have to do is walk north several hundred yards to a more secluded spot. The beach is a mile long and often deserted on the north end.

6 Petoskey State Park

2475 M-119, Petoskey 49770; (231) 347-2311
tinyurl.com/petoskeystatepark

Little Traverse Bay is famous for its quaint coastal communities, and the beauty of the bay is why they are here. Enjoy the western expanse of the bay from Petoskey State Park and catch a sunset or two. Perfect for painters, collectors of Petoskey stones (see page 143), swimmers, or sunbathers, this is a convenient park for locals and tourists alike. Even before you sit down to enjoy the sunset, you can enjoy the varying colors created by the sun reflecting off the bay If you want to take a bike ride, a trail connects the park to the town of Petoskey.

7 Pictured Rocks National Lakeshore

Munising Falls Visitor Center (open year-round) 1505 Sand Point Road, Munising 49862; (906) 387-3700

Grand Sable Visitor Center (open summer only) E21090 County Road H-58, Seney; (906) 494-2660
nps.gov/piro

Pictured Rocks National Lakeshore is included in several different sections of this book, and for good reason: there is simply so much to see and do there. The beaches are just one reason to visit. Walking the rugged Twelvemile Beach is a pleasure. Whether it is the breeze and waves, the shorebirds, or signs of old shipwrecks, this beach is pristine and protected. If the word *unspoiled* was ever appropriate for a beach, this is it. There is also a long beach beneath the Grand Sable Dunes, as well as high, perched bluffs. Surprisingly, this beach is rocky and a wonderful place to look at beach cobbles. There are nine beaches in total, though some require lengthy hikes to access (see nps.gov/piro/planyourvisit/dayhikes.htm for more information). If you visit, be aware that removing rocks and other natural features from Pictured Rocks is prohibited.

Port Crescent State Park

1775 Port Austin Road, Port Austin 48467; (989) 738-8663
tinyurl.com/portcrescentstatepark

Though less popular than Lake Michigan, Lake Huron also has its share of beautiful beaches—and they are often less crowded than those on the west side of the state. This park has 3 miles of sandy beach on the sheltered Saginaw Bay. In addition to the shallow waters and sandy shore, there are opportunities for fishing, canoeing, hiking, cross-country skiing, birding, and hunting. If you or your family desire more sand and sun, there is a boardwalk with lots of scenic views to find and enjoy. Stay past dark to take advantage of the park's dark-sky preserve, which will let you view the stars without light pollution.

Redwyn Dunes Nature Sanctuary

Sand Dunes Drive, Mohawk 49950; (866) 223-2231
tinyurl.com/redwyndunes

This place is something different. This isn't designed for recreation, but rather as a sanctuary where you can sincerely contemplate and interact with nature. Here you can relax and take in the mile-long trail, the stable dunes, and the woods of red oak and pine. If you go, bring a camera or your art supplies, write in a journal or be a naturalist. You wouldn't be the first: the dunes are named after *The Lost History of Redwyn,* by William J. Skora, who was inspired by the beauty of this place.

Silver Lake State Park

9679 W. State Park Road, Mears 49436; (231) 873-3083
tinyurl.com/silverlakestatepark

In this book, we often emphasize trips that offer quiet and solitude, but this site is the exception. This 2,000-acre sand area allows off-road-vehicle (ORV) drivers to test their skills—in fact, these are the only sand dunes open to ORVs east of the Mississippi River. But the park is divided into several sections, and not all the dunes are open to off-road drivers. The central portion of the park is reserved for hiking, walking, and simple beach activities; the north area is open for ORV dune rides; and the southern portion is the home of **Mac Wood's Dune Rides** (macwoodsdunerides.com), which provide tours of the dunes for the whole family. ORV rentals are also available; see the website for details.

11 Sleeping Bear Dunes National Lakeshore

Philip A. Hart Visitor Center 9922 W. Front St., Empire 49630;
(231) 326-4700, ext. 5010
nps.gov/slbe

How can you go wrong with the place that was voted the "Most Beautiful Place in America" by the viewers of *Good Morning America*? With 35 miles of pristine beach, the huge perched dunes, and deep blue waters of Lake Michigan, this is a summer paradise. The dunes are the highlight, of course, but give yourself time to see some of the other sites as well, including rivers, trails, and inland lakes. If history is more your thing, visit Port Oneida Rural Historic District or the Maritime Museum And if you want to get even more off the beaten path, there are miles more of beaches on North and South Manitou Island, which are accessible by ferry.

12 South Haven Beaches

Water Street, North Shore Drive, and Lakeshore Drive, South Haven 49090;
(269) 637-0772
southhaven.org/experience/beaches-and-waters

There are eight beaches to choose from. Yes, you read right—eight! The beaches on the northern and southern ends seem to be the largest (and busiest), and they include concession stands, parking, and restrooms. You can also play volleyball, have a picnic, set up your grill, or just relax. Packard Beach offers similar options, while others specialize in sunsets and sand only. Children (or those young at heart) will also find a skateboard park, a splash pad, an aqua sports complex at South Haven, and a pier that invites you to take an evening stroll. Like at all the dunes and beaches, there are myriad options if you choose to leave the sand, walk, explore, and get exercise. Come during June to get some U-pick strawberries.

13 Sterling State Park

2800 State Park Road, Monroe 48162; (734) 289-2715
tinyurl.com/sterlingstatepark

Amid all of the Great Lakes and their extremely long shorelines, it's often easy to forget Lake Erie, but that'd be a mistake. Located in th southeast portion of the state, William C. Sterling State Park is easy to access, and with a mile-long beach, boat launches, fishing lagoons, campsites, and picnic areas, there's a lot to do. The wildlife-viewing trails are an especially good diversion, and the River Raisin National Battlefield Park (see page 120) can be reached by a hiking trail from the park.

Van Buren State Park

23960 Ruggles Road, South Haven 49090; (269) 637-2788
tinyurl.com/vanburenstatepark

Not far from South Haven and its many beaches, this small state park has high dunes and a campground, along with picnicking, hiking, and biking in addition to beach options. A state trail passes through the park and is perfect for hiking and biking. The beach here is not particularly large, but it's a great place to relax, and one that's still close to the shops and excitement of South Haven's tourist area. Come in the winter for skiing and snowmobiling and see the park all over again.

Warren Dunes State Park

12032 Red Arrow Highway, Sawyer 49125; (269) 426-4013
tinyurl.com/warrendunesstatepark

This park features 3 miles of beaches that are wonderful places to play, run in the sand, or simply sunbathe on the shores of Lake Michigan. But it is the dunes themselves that will eventually draw you here. These are so large that they have been given names (not unlike mountain peaks), and some of the dunes are popular for sandboarding. If you need an escape from sun and surf, consider walking along a shaded hiking trail or exploring the flora of the dunes. This is one of the most popular beaches in Michigan, so be prepared for a crowd in some places. There are picnicking and camping facilities here, too.

Wilderness State Park

903 Wilderness Park Drive, Carp Lake 49718; (231) 436-5381
tinyurl.com/wildernessstatepark

The beaches at Wilderness State Park are on the upper northwest shoulder of the Lower Peninsula, in a wild and remote area. These are not the soft sand beaches of the south. The shoreline consists of a mix of conifers and hardwoods, and there are rocks and driftwood present in some places; if you're looking for solitude, come here. There are even rustic cabins so you can make this a Northwoods getaway. The park is also quite large—over 10,000 acres—with inland lakes and trails to explore when you're not enjoying the waves and beaches. All told, this might be the best wilderness experience on the Lake Michigan shore.

Mushroom Houses of Charlevoix

THE HISTORY OF A CIVILIZATION is reflected, in part, in the buildings it creates. From mushroom houses to Calumet Theatre, the architecture of Michigan is as diverse as its landscape and history. Exploring these locations is a great way to learn about the state's history.

HISTORIC BUILDINGS & ARCHITECTURE

(continued on next page)

e historic Mission Church in Mackinaw City

1 Calumet Theatre

340 Sixth St., Calumet 49913; (906) 337-2610
calumettheatre.com

The Calumet Theatre, a National Historic Landmark, represents the age of the copper boom of the late 19th and early 20th centuries, when the town was flourishing and could afford world-class live entertainment; the theatre then became a movie house during the early days of the film industry. Having operated continuously since 1900, the Calumet still hosts a variety of movies and live shows. Elaborately designed, the building is a two-story Renaissance Reviva structure, and the stone exterior is the gorgeous and multicolored Jacobsville sandstone. Highlights also include a copper roof, a clock, and a bell tower. The exterior of the theater represents the efforts of local architect Charles K. Shand, while the elaborate interior was cre ated by Chicago designer William Eckert.

2 Detroit Historic Districts

Numerous locations throughout Detroit; see website below for an interactive map
detroitmi.gov/webapp/local-historic-district-map

Detroit has done something that every city needs to do: it has recog nized its distinct neighborhoods and celebrated each area's specific history, architecture, and residents—everything that has helped cor tribute to making the neighborhoods unique and memorable. Each district has its own historic buildings and architectural designs and is worth exploring by car, foot, bike, or public transport. Detroit's neighborhoods are a reminder that cities are an agglomeration of developments, and they often grow by absorbing other existing com munities. You can't see all of the districts in one day, but they are worthy of day trips with stops at local bars, restaurants, and other public places; see experiencedetroit.com/historicneighborhoods. htm for a sample tour, or search online for "Detroit historical tours, "Detroit neighborhood tours," "Detroit walking tours," and the like.

Earl Young Mushroom Houses

Park Avenue, Clinton Street, Grant Street, Lake Shore Drive, Boulder Avenue, Eastern Road, Western Road, and Lakeview Avenue, Charlevoix 49720

Brochure/map available at Charlevoix Visitor Bureau, 109 Mason St., Charlevoix 49720; (800) 367-8557, 231-547-2101, tinyurl.com/earlyoungbrochure
self-guided tour available at minivanadventures.com/charlevoix-mushroom-houses

Earl Young's unique Mushroom Houses have been called a variety of things: weird, quirky, whimsical, hobbit houses, gnome homes, fairy-tale homes, imagination dwellings, unforgettable houses! You have to take a walk in the Charlevoix neighborhoods where this world-famous group of homes can be found. Most of these homes are private dwellings, but if you want to turn your day trip into a multiday trip, a few of the houses are available to rent. From 1918 to the 1970s, Young, who was self-taught, designed 30 stone homes using materials found in northern Michigan, and each one is a unique work of art. With stone walls capped by mushroom-like cedar roofs, windows outlined by boulders, and chimneys and doorways framed by large stones, these are sights to behold. The best way to experience these houses is to simply take a walk on the sidewalk; just remember that while maps and descriptions are readily available for visitors, these are still private residences.

Fox Theatre

2211 Woodward Ave., Detroit 48201; (313) 471-3200
313presents.com/fox-theatre

The Fox Theatre is part of District Detroit, an entertainment and sports area in downtown Detroit. The flagship of what was once a national chain, it opened in 1928 and was the first movie theater in the world built with equipment for showing sound pictures. Over the years it has been visited by a host of big names, including Elvis Presley and Shirley Temple. The entertainment on stage isn't all there is to see here, however: the building is a sight all its own. The architecture is Hindu-Thai-Byzantine, a conglomeration of Far Eastern, Egyptian, and Indian themes from various eras. The architect, C. Howard Crane, designed over 250 theaters across the country, but the Fox Theatre in Detroit is considered by many to be his greatest work. This theater is on the National Register of Historic Places and is a National Historic Landmark.

6 Various locations

5 Heritage Hill: A National, State, and Local Historic District

Heritage Hill Association, 126 College Ave. SE, Grand Rapids 49503; (616) 459-8950
heritagehillweb.org

This neighborhood of 1,300 homes and businesses is Michigan's largest and finest collection of 19th- and 20th-century American architecture. Dating back to 1844, much of this neighborhood was slated for demolition in the 1960s due to a variety of urban renewal developments in area. Residents formed the Heritage Hill Association and worked diligently to place Heritage Hill on the National Register of Historic Places, which halted all plans for demolition and redevelopment. It is a wonderful example of how residents with pride can preserve their community for both today and tomorrow. Self-guided walking tour information is available at the website. An annual Weekend Tour of Homes is held the third weekend in May, and a garden tour is held each summer. Lovers of Frank Lloyd Wright architecture will also appreciate seeing the Meyer May House, which Wright designed in the early 1900s. The house is open to the public only a few days each week, however, so plan your visit wisely.

6 Historic Churches of Michigan

The Cathedral Church of St Paul Built 1908; parish founded 1824.
4800 Woodward Ave., Detroit 48201; (313) 831-5000
detroitcathedral.org

Cathedral of Saint Andrew Built 1875.
215 Sheldon Blvd. SE, Grand Rapids 49503; (616) 456-1454
cathedralofsaintandrew.org

First Congregational Church of Detroit Built 1891; parish founded 1844.
33 E. Forest Ave., Detroit 48201; (313) 831-4080
friendsoffirst.com/about-us

Historic King Solomon Baptist Church Built 1951; congregation founded 1926
6100 14th St., Detroit 48208; (313) 355-2150
kingsolomonchurch.org

Historic Mission Church Built 1830; now a museum. *Note:* Has barriers to accessibility.
Main Street, Mackinaw City 49701; (906) 847-3328
mackinacparks.com

Historic Trinity Lutheran Church First built 1866; current building dates from 1931.
1345 Gratiot Ave., Detroit 48207; (313) 567-3100
historictrinity.org

Old Rugged Cross Church Built (as a barn) in 1862; converted to a church in 1876;
renovated in 1998.
61041 Vermont St., Pokagon Township 49047; (269) 683-4540
the-oldruggedcross.org

Omena Presbyterian Church Built 1858; open during summer.
5098 N. West Bay Shore Drive (PO Box 187), Omena 49674
omenachurch.org

Second Baptist Church of Detroit Built 1914; congregation founded in 1836; was a
stop on the Underground Railroad (see page 116); has operated in the same location
since 1857.
441 Monroe St., Detroit 48226; (313) 961-0920
secondbaptistdetroit.org

Ste. Anne Catholic Church Originally built in 1743 in Mackinaw City; dismantled
and moved to Mackinac Island in 1780; current building dates from 1873; baptismal
records date back to 1695.
Main St., Mackinac Island; (231) 847-3507
steanneschurch.org

Ste. Anne de Detroit Built 1886; parish founded 1701.
1000 St. Anne St., Detroit 48216; (313) 496-1701
ste-anne.org

St. Florian Church Originally built 1908; rebuilt 1926.
2626 Poland St., Hamtramck 48212; (313) 871-2778
stflorianparish.org

St. John the Evangelist Church Built 1856.
711 N. Martin Luther King Jr. Drive, Jackson 49201; (517) 784-0553
stjohnjackson.org

St. Joseph Shrine Built 1873.
1828 Jay St., Detroit 48207; (313) 831-6659
institute-christ-king.org/detroit

St. Mary Roman Catholic Church Built 1911.
210 W. Main St., Manchester 48158; (734) 428-8811
stmarymanchester.org

St. Paul the Apostle Church Built 1908.
301 Eighth St., Calumet 49913; (906) 337-0810
keweenawcc.org, dioceseofmarquette.org/stpaulcalumet

Hoyt Public Library

505 Janes Ave., Saginaw 48607; (989) 755-0904
saginawlibrary.org/branch/hoyt-main

This is one of the most impressive buildings in all of Michigan. A gift
of lumber baron Jesse Hoyt to the City of Saginaw, this elaborate
structure was designed by the architectural firm of Van Brunt and
Howe of Boston after a nationwide competition was held in 1890. An
eye-catching building, the library features limestone blocks from Bay
Port's quarry and a trim of red sandstone from Lake Superior quarries.

8 Lakeshore Museum Center

430 W. Clay Ave., Muskegon 49440; (231) 722-0278
lakeshoremuseum.org

This museum doesn't just have traditional indoor exhibits—it also has historic buildings. The museum itself has permanent and changing exhibits that explore the natural and cultural history of the area, but make sure you visit all five museum structures. The Hackley and Hume Homes, formerly occupied by lumber barons, showcase some of the finest examples of Queen Anne–style Victorian homes in the country. Designed by David S. Hopkins of Grand Rapids and built in the late 1880s, they feature lavish woodcarvings, stenciling, stained glass windows, and period furnishings. The Scolnik House of the Depression Era, with period furnishings and appliances, highlights family life during the Great Depression. Finally, the history of firefighting is told at the Fire Barn Museum. This re-creation of a firehouse from the late 1800s includes hose carts, hook-and-ladder trucks, uniforms, and photographs of some of the area's most devastating fires.

9 Meadow Brook Hall

480 South Adams Road, Rochester 48309; (248) 364-6200
meadowbrookhall.org

A classic example of Tudor Revival architecture modeled after English country manors, this was the home of Matilda Dodge Wilson, widow of one of Dodge Brothers Motor Company's co-founders. Wilson, who was actively involved in both the interior and exterior design of the house, took pride in the fact that the house consisted mostly of American-made materials. Finished in 1929, the house's 88,000 square feet and 110 rooms make it one of the largest homes in the Midwest. For art lovers, the Hall includes a collection of the art Wilson accumulated over the years.

Michigan State Capitol

100 Capitol Ave., Lansing 48933; (517) 373-2353
capitol.michigan.gov; *walking tour:* council.legislature.mi.gov/content/files/tours
/capinfo.pdf

Michigan trivia lovers know that the first capitol in Michigan was built
in Detroit, but less well known is the fact that Michigan's present
capitol building is actually the third building that has served as the
state's capitol. The current building, designed by Elijah E. Myers, took
six years to complete and opened on New Year's Day of 1879. The
building, constructed in the Renaissance Revival style, includes many
interesting faux finishes, including pine painted to mimic walnut and
cast iron that mimics marble. The building still contains many of its
original elements, including the black-and-white Vermont limestone
and marble floors, as well as an 976-glass-tile floor in the capitol's
rotunda. A beautiful cast-iron-and-tin dome soars above, decorated
with stars and muses that show the way to Michigan's future, inspiring
citizens and visitors alike. Art lovers will also appreciate the 9 acres of
surface space that is decorated with hand-painted art.

The State Capitol building in Lansing

11 Osceola Quilt Trail

Various locations in Osceola Country
For a guide and map, send a self-addressed stamped envelope to PO Box 301, Tustin 49688
sites.google.com/site/osceolaquiltrail

Following the lead of quilt trails in other states, the Osceola Quilt Trail is the result of a creative effort by businesses, residents, and barn owners to decorate buildings with quilt designs. It's not the architecture here that is important, but rather the painted quilting designs and patterns. This trail is a fun way to explore the rural landscape and forms a type of scavenger hunt. From quilt-bedecked barns to post offices, the quilt trail has stops in Marion, Tustin, LeRoy, Hersey, Evart, and Reed City. While visible from the road, most quilt blocks adorn private structures, though more than a dozen grace the sides of public buildings.

12 Superior Dome

Northern Michigan University 1401 Presque Isle Ave., Marquette 49855-5301; (906) 227-1000
nmu.edu/superiordome

In 2010, the Superior Dome, home of Northern Michigan University's football, soccer, and track teams, set a world record as the world's fifth-largest dome (by diameter) and the world's largest wooden dome structure. To give you an idea of how big it is, there are 781 Douglas-fir beams supporting this massive roof. In a place known for intense winters, this geodesic dome supports up to 60 pounds per square foot of snow and can withstand winds of up to 80 miles per hour. The stadium also has retractable artificial turf, which means the dome can be used for a wide variety of activities and events.

3 Thumb Octagon Barn Agricultural Museum

6948 Richie Road, Gagetown 48735; (989) 665-0081
thumboctagonbarn.org

James Luther Purdy bought the land where this barn stands in 1895 with the goal of building an octagonal barn. He had first seen this style of barn when in Iowa and wanted to bring the design to his own farm complex, and in 1923, he achieved this goal. Each of the eight sides of the barn is 42 feet wide by 24 feet high, and the very tip of the structure is 70 feet above the ground. Though the barn is definitely the highlight here, it's not the only period building to see: other restored or reconstructed structures include a sawmill, a covered bridge, a blacksmith shop, a cider mill, and a one-room schoolhouse. Demonstrations and special events are common at the barn, so bring your whole family to learn about early-20th-century agriculture.

4 William G. Thompson House Museum and Gardens

101 Summit St., Hudson 49247; (517) 448-8125
thompsonmuseum.org

This Queen Anne–style home, built in 1890, looks nearly the same as it did on the day William G. Thompson last occupied the house. The exterior features include bay windows, a turret, a metal roof, and a cut-stone foundation. Inside, find art, antiques, and Thompson's personal papers. The gardens, including a privet hedge, are an integral part of a visit. A large copper beech tree is a landmark for the location, and the roses are a delight of summer color. With all of this history and beauty, it's no wonder the house is listed on the National Register of Historic Places.

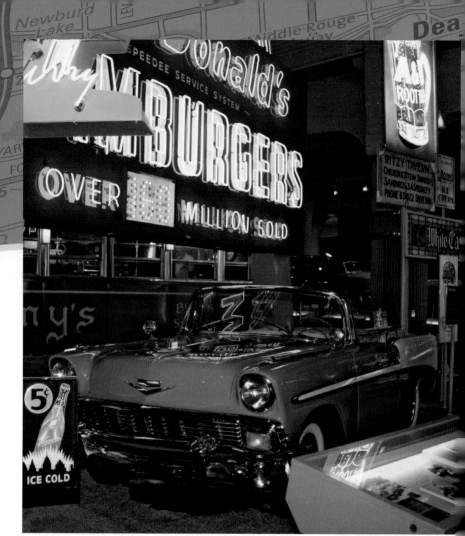

Henry Ford Museum

IF YOU WERE TO LIST THE 50 STATES in a word-association game, Michigan would be too easy. Yes, it is the Peninsula State, and yes, it is the Great Lakes State, but most of all it is the Auto State. Mention Detroit and, for many people, it's not the Tigers, Red Wings, Pistons, or Lions that come to mind first, it's the automobiles—specifically Ford, Chrysler, and General Motors. Michigan is the epicenter of everything automotive, and there are opportunities to explore auto history throughout the state.

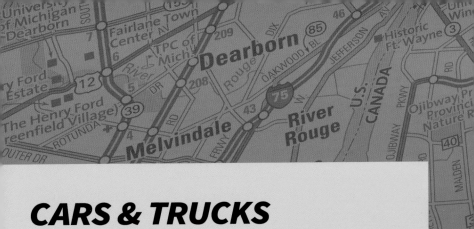

CARS & TRUCKS

(continued on next page)

If you like cars, you're in the right state

1 Automotive Hall of Fame

21400 Oakwood Blvd., Dearborn 48124; (313) 240-4000
automotivehalloffame.org

The automobile has become more than an American icon; it is an essential part of both our economy and social world—and people in Michigan have often had a front-row seat to the industry's development. This museum about automotive pioneers and innovators is not limited to Michigan history, though; it tells stories of automobile old-timers from around the globe. Here, important stories that are often lost to the current generation can be found, such as the tale of Alice Ramsey, the first woman to drive across the country, along with background about Zora Arkus-Duntov, who is forever linked to the Corvette. The displays and exhibits, as well as the individuals who are honored, present a fascinating history of the car. Visit the Hall of Honor to see the history of the automobile immortalized in a 11-by-65-foot mural made up of 90 individual images.

2 Brockway Mountain Drive

Copper Harbor 49918; Keweenaw Convention & Visitors Bureau, (800) 338-7982, (906) 337-4579
copperharbor.org/things-to-do/scenic-drives

Located on the northern tip of the Keweenaw Peninsula, Brockway Mountain Drive is a wonderful drive noted for its scenery and lovely setting. This uphill drive of nearly 10 miles offers some of the most stunning views of Lake Superior and the harbor at Copper Harbor—and, if the weather cooperates, you might even be able to see Isle Royale. This is the highest paved drive above sea level between the Rockies and the Alleghenies. Make sure to stop at some of the many pull-offs so the driver can take in the views, too. To add to its appeal, this is also an official Michigan Wildlife Viewing Area. (*Note:* Closed in winter.)

Byways to Flyways

Detroit River International Wildlife Refuge Large Lakes Research Station, 9311 Groh Road, Grosse Ile 48138; (734) 365-0219
tinyurl.com/bywaystoflyways

Combining a driving tour and a bird-watching trip is a great idea. Centering a bird-watching trip on the diverse habitats of the Detroit River and western Lake Erie ensures both a variety of scenery and an abundance of species to spot. Two of the four great flyways of the continent converge here, and up to 350 species have been recorded. There are 27 birding sites along this route and eight Important Birding Areas. Besides the region's many songbirds, waterfowl, and shorebirds are common here. The edge of the forest is a route for raptors that prefer to avoid flying over open water. Check the website for information on what birds you're likely to see at different locations during different seasons.

Ford Piquette Avenue Plant (Birthplace of the Model T)

461 Piquette Ave., Detroit 48202; (313) 872-8759
fordpiquetteplant.org

Is there a car that is more famous or more iconic than the Model T? It was not the first car created, but it was the first mass-produced car with replaceable parts. The age of the automobile truly began when Ford Motor Company established its first purpose-built factory here in 1904. Eventually, this plant would go on to be used by other companies for other purposes, but shortly after the turn of the 20th century it was restored. Today, it is an independent museum of early automobiles and exhibits Studebakers, Hupmobiles, and other now-obscure brands in addition to Fords. You can also see Henry Ford's office here.

Ford Rouge Factory Tour

The Henry Ford 20900 Oakwood Blvd., Dearborn 48124-5029; (800) 835-5237, (313) 982-6001
thehenryford.org/visit/ford-rouge-factory-tour

While technically part of the Henry Ford Museum, discussed on page 74, this experience deserves an entry all its own. This self-guided tour takes visitors behind the scenes of Ford manufacturing; from two theaters to an observation deck and a gallery that add information, background, and a little dramatics to your visit, there is lots to see and do here. There were originally 93 active buildings in this complex. With ore docks, steel furnaces, rolling mills, glass furnaces, and even their own power plant, Ford controlled the entire process, from raw materials to finished products. At one time more than 100,000 people worked at the plant. If you want to experience this tour, park at the main Henry Ford Museum campus and catch the shuttle to the factory.

Cars & Trucks

6 Gilmore Car Museum

6865 Hickory Road, Hickory Corners 49060; (269) 671-5089
gilmorecarmuseum.org

What began as one man's passion has today become the largest museum dedicated to the automobile in all of North America. Donald S. Gilmore's wife, Genevieve, had the idea to turn her husband's collection into a museum that could be enjoyed by all ages, and so the Gilmore Car Museum was born. Entering the main exhibit hall and the 90-acre historic campus is breathtaking. The Automobile Heritage Center has more than 400 cars on display, which is likely to make it hard for you to find a favorite. There is also a 1930s service station, vintage pedal cars, and the Blue Moon Silk City 1941 Diner. A motorcycle collection and even nostalgia pieces (such as the collection of hood ornaments) are additional treats. In the summer, numerous events and car shows make this museum an experience for a full day or even a weekend.

7 The Henry Ford Museum of American Innovation

20900 Oakwood Blvd., Dearborn 48124-5029; (313) 982-6001
thehenryford.org

This museum is so large that you need to take breaks for food, maybe a film, or even a visit to the Rouge Factory or Greenfield Village (see pages 73 and 118). Then it's time to return and see more. The museum rightfully boasts of housing 26 million artifacts, which means you're *not* going to see everything in one visit, but this museum is always worth returning to. This is history as told through the windshield of our automobiles. Many of the exhibits, such as the Oscar Mayer Wienermobile, are lighthearted. Others, such as the limo that JFK rode in when he was shot and the bus where Rosa Parks made her courageous stand, are more emotional. Make sure to give yourself plenty of time when you visit.

8 Highway 41 Historic Road Trip

US 41, Upper Peninsula to Florida
michiganhighways.org/listings/US-041.html

US 41 is a fascinating option for drivers who prefer to experience the road than to learn about it in a museum. This national highway runs north to south and begins at a cul-de-sac near Fort Wilkins and Copper Harbor and doesn't stop until it gets to Miami, Florida. The route traverses over 250 miles of the U.P. and enters Wisconsin at the Menominee River. The towns along the route from Copper Harbor to Menominee include Escanaba, Rapid River, Marquette, L'Anse, Houghton, and Hancock.

Michigan International Speedway

12626 US 12, Brooklyn 49230-9068; (517) 592-6666
mispeedway.com

Home to one of the largest single-day sporting events in the state, this is Michigan's home for automobile racing. At 2 miles long, the Speedway has one of the lengthiest tracks in all of NASCAR. That's not all its known for, however: with its wide turns and consistently fast averages for qualifying speeds, it is known as the "fastest track in NASCAR." For those interested in packing in a weekend of fun around the various races, various camping opportunities are available at or near the track.

Pierce Stocking Scenic Drive

Sleeping Bear Dunes National Lakeshore Philip A. Hart Visitor Center, 9922 Front St., Empire 49630; (231) 326-4700
nps.gov/slbe/planyourvisit/psscenicdrive.htm

This drive was named for Pierce Stocking, a lumberman who created the road in the 1960s to share his love of the area's beauty. Located within Sleeping Bear Dunes National Lakeshore, this 7.4-mile drive is located between Empire and Glen Arbor. Large sand dunes, forests, inland lakes, and Lake Michigan's shores are among the highlights for bikers and drivers, and you should feel free to stop and see some of the scenic vistas and short hikes along the drive. Popular stops and sights along the drive include Little and Big Glen Lakes, Lake Michigan's Manitou Islands, Lake Michigan's Sleeping Bear Bay, and the Observation Deck at Lake Michigan. Markers along the drive provide insights into the history and scenery of the area, and visitors are also encouraged to pick up a guide to the route at the Hart Visitor Center in Empire.

R. E. Olds Transportation Museum

240 Museum Drive, Lansing 48933; (517) 372-0529
reoldsmuseum.org

Lansing is the birthplace of the Oldsmobile, but Ransom Eli Olds and the Lansing area have given more to the transportation world than just the classic automobile. Olds also designed lawn mowers, including their engines, both through his Ideal Engine Company and

through REO Motors. At the height of the company's success, REO was the largest producer of power lawn mowers in the entire world. Of course, you'll also find many connections to the automobile industry here, with the history of the Olds Motor Works, the REO Motor Car Company, and the story of R. E. Olds himself. Engines, automobiles, and other memorabilia make this a stop to remember.

12 River Road National Scenic Byway

Huron National Forest M-65 and River Road from Hale to Oscoda; (231) 775-2421
tinyurl.com/riverroadscenicbyway

This 22-mile drive through Huron National Forest winds past forests and along streams to Oscoda, near Lake Huron. Along the way, views of the Au Sable River (see page 10) will tempt you to put in a canoe, and that's just one of the recreational opportunities available along the route. There's also hiking, cross-country skiing, fishing, hunting, and bird-watching. In Oscoda, visit the Lumberman's Monument and stop in at the visitor center, which will connect you with the lumber industry's past. An interpretive site at Largo Springs will take you, via boardwalk, to a spectacular view of the Largo Springs and the river below.

13 Sloan Museum Buick Automotive Gallery and Research Center

Courtland Center Mall 4190 E. Court St., Burton 48509; (810) 237-3450
sloanlongway.org/automotive-collection

Buick was founded in Detroit as the Buick Auto-Vim and Power Company in 1899 before becoming the Buick Motor Company and moving to Flint in 1903, then becoming a division of General Motors in 1908. The history of the Buick can be explored through archives and photos as well as a collection of Buicks on display in the Sloan Museum. There are usually around 30 automobiles on display.

14 Stahls Automotive Foundation

56516 N. Bay Drive, Chesterfield 48051; (586) 749-1078
stahlsauto.com

This is an excellent collection of vintage cars, gas pumps, road signs and other automobile-related artifacts. The cars in this collection are based on engineering innovation and excellence, and every era of automotive history is on display here—from the 1886 Daimler to the muscle cars of the 1960s. If someone in your party is not interested in cars, they have a large collection of antique musical instruments, too.

5 Whitefish Bay National Forest Scenic Byway

Paradise to Brimley
tinyurl.com/whitefishbayscenicbyway

Whitefish Bay National Forest Scenic Byway is in Hiawatha National Forest in the U.P. This 30-mile route is parallel to the North Country National Scenic Trail (see page17), which makes it a good place to combine walking and driving so as to get the most out of the scenery. The hiking trail is in good shape here, and nearby Lake Superior is a beautiful vivid blue. Popular stops along the route include the overlook at Naomikong Creek, the Point Iroquois Lighthouse, and the gorgeous shallow waters of Tahquamenon Bay. Some of the stops on this trip are closed in the winter months.

6 Woodward Avenue Dream Cruise

Woodward Avenue, Detroit
woodwarddreamcruise.com

The Motor City is the perfect place for the Dream Cruise: originally a soccer fundraiser, this event has become one of the premier car cruises in the world. Today, more than 1.5 million spectators enjoy seeing 40,000 classic cars drive down Woodward Avenue, "America's first highway." The route also visits the sites of classic 1950s-era Detroit restaurants ("Drivin' from Drive-In to Drive-In"). So get in the car, turn on the rock and roll, roll down your bobby socks, and cruise.

7 Ypsilanti Automotive Heritage Museum

100 E. Cross St., Ypsilanti 48197; (734) 482-5200
ypsiautoheritage.org

Not only does this museum have a wonderful collection of cars from several now-extinct car brands, such as Hudson and Kaiser-Frazer, but it's also the home of the National Hudson Motor Car Company Museum. Some highlights include the 1933 Hudson Terraplane K Series Coach and a 1952 Hudson Hornet NASCAR champion driven by Herb Thomas—his story provided the inspiration for the 2006 Pixar film *Cars*. The museum also has vintage advertising and promotional materials. If you want even more to do in one day, check out the **Michigan Firehouse Museum** (michiganfirehousemuseum.org), just two blocks away.

Grand Hotel on Mackinac Island

ONLY YOU CAN DETERMINE what makes for a romantic or fun getaway, as the terms can be so subjective. Sometimes it's just a quiet place to watch the sunset or a view of a bay filled with sailboats, or it could be a lively party at a pool. All the places in this section have a sense of place that contrasts strongly with our busy daily lives—and with a wide variety of places to choose from, there should be something here for everyone.

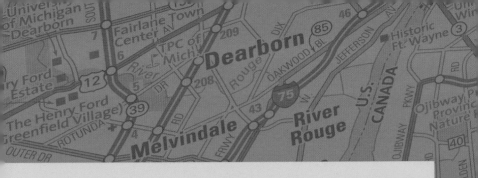

FUN GETAWAYS

(continued on next page)

The Holz-Brücke (German for Wooden Bridge) near Frankenmuth, which has long ties to Germany

1 Castle in the Country Bed & Breakfast Inn

340 M-40 S., Allegan 49010; (269) 673-8054
castleinthecountry.com

This refurbished Victorian mansion offers themed rooms for your romantic getaway. With suites, whirlpools, and fireplaces, this 10-room inn provides all the amenities, including kayaks and paddleboats that visitors can use on the private lake. The wooded trails wind through the forest and are great places to exercise and reflect. Side-by-side massages are a nice option for couples.

2 Chateau Chantal

15900 Rue de Vin, Traverse City 49686; (800) 969-4009, (231) 223-4110
chateauchantal.com

In an attempt to offer the ideal experience, Chateau Chantal has created many packages visitors can choose from. A wine-pairing/dinner package is just one of the special options you can consider. Situated on a peninsula, the château sits amid a sea of fruit trees and vines and is removed from the noise and energy of Traverse City, providing a quiet place to get away. When coupled with the gleaming water of Grand Traverse Bay, the 65 acres surrounding the château are perfect for photography, painting, or simple relaxation. If you're staying at the inn, the tasting room is close to the guest rooms, and there is a variety of wine to choose from. Cooking classes are offered as well, with dates available at the website.

3 Crystal Mountain

12500 Crystal Mountain Drive, Thompsonville 49683; (855) 995-5146
crystalmountain.com

A destination for the entire family, this resort is a great place to be any time of the year. In summer, it offers 36 holes of golf, indoor and outdoor pools, tennis courts, mountain biking, and Michigan's only Alpine slide. In winter, it features downhill and cross-country skiing, ice skating, and snowshoeing. Visitors can enjoy some amenities year-round, such as the fitness center, Michigan Legacy Art Park, and the Crystal Spa, which emphasizes renewal and relaxation with a variety of spa services. Even better, the resort is LEED-certified as environmentally friendly, honoring the beauty of northern Michigan in a mountain oasis.

4 Garden Grove Bed & Breakfast

9549 Union Pier Road, Union Pier 49129; (800) 613-2872, (269) 469-6346
gardengrove.net

Located in Harbor Country and close to Warren Dunes State Park, this is a wonderful option for experiencing cottage living. Close to Chicago, but far enough away to be a true escape, this bed and breakfast is a popular destination for weddings and anniversaries. Nearby communities offer beaches, restaurants, golf courses, and shopping, while the rooms will encourage you to lounge and relax. A casino, a local wine trail, and microbreweries offer more options.

5 Grand Hotel

286 Grand Ave., Mackinac Island 49757; (800) 334-7263 (reservations), (906) 847-3331 (general hotel information)
grandhotel.com

Is it the island setting, the lack of cars, the historic furnishings, the grandeur of the building, the Hollywood connection, or the world-famous surroundings that make this 1887 hotel so popular and in demand? *Travel + Leisure* magazine lists it as one of the top 500 hotels in the world. Every visit here is different, as each room is slightly different. Whichever room you stay in, the rocking chairs on the "world's largest porch" beckon and are one of the most inviting places for reading and relaxation in Michigan. Held in late October, the Grand's *Somewhere in Time* Weekend celebrates the hotel's prominent role in the beloved movie classic and features a screening of the film, panel discussions led by cast and crew members, and a period-costume promenade. One warning before you go: there are modern conveniences, but nothing about the overall hotel is modern except, of course, for the prices. *Note:* There is a dress code at the Grand, so make sure to check the website for more information before you visit.

The Heather House Bed & Breakfast

409 N. Main St., Marine City 48039; (810) 765-3175
theheatherhouse.com

This 1888 Queen Anne Victorian house overlooks the St. Clair River, which is connected to the St. Lawrence Seaway. This means that as you sit and relax at this beautiful bed and breakfast, you can watch upbound and downbound river traffic pass by, from freighters to sailboats. With private bathrooms and outdoor porches, the bed-and-breakfast ensures you'll enjoy your stay in privacy and comfort. Take some time to explore the local town, too. There's dining, a few

museums, antiques shops, and a host of outdoor activities. If you have your passport on you, take the ferry over to Sombra, Ontario, for additional things to do.

7 The Historic Webster House

900 Fifth St., Bay City 48708; (989) 316-2552, (877) 229-9704
historicwebsterhouse.com

This Queen Anne Victorian house is located in Bay City's historic district, just a few blocks from the waterfront. The interior of this 1886 house has been renovated to meet the highest standards of elegance and style. Popular for weddings and other events, this bed-and-breakfast is a getaway for honeymooners and romantic travelers of all ages. It features European-style feather-top queen-size beds and down duvets to snuggle into. A formal dining room creates the ideal setting for breakfasts and other special meals. Plan your getaway to correspond with one of the local festivals to further enhance the trip.

8 The Homestead

1 Wood Ridge Road, Glen Arbor 49636; (231) 334-5000, (231) 228-6000 (golfing tee times)
thehomesteadresort.com

With a spa that sits on a ridge overlooking Lake Michigan and the pristine landscape of Sleeping Bear Bay and the Manitou Islands, this resort is a setting fit for reflection, tranquility, and meditation in surrounding terraces, gardens, and labyrinths. If you seek other escapes, swimming, biking, hiking, sailing, and other outdoor options are available. When it comes to dining at the resort, like everything else at The Homestead, it's meant to make your vacation memorable. That means fresh ingredients, locally sourced when possible. It means stunning settings, with friendly, professional service. After dinner, hit the links nearby, with 18 holes all featuring views of Lake Michigan.

9 The Inn at Bay Harbor

3600 Village Harbor Drive, Bay Harbor 49770-8577; (231) 439-4000
innatbayharbor.com

Travel + Leisure magazine named this luxury resort one of "The World's Best Hotels." Owned by Marriott, the sprawling resort is associated with a championship golf course and has a day spa. The real treat, however, is the resort's location on Lake Michigan, which gives this already-special resort a stunning backdrop.

0 Inn at Black Star Farms

10844 E. Revold Road, Suttons Bay 49682; (231) 944-1251
blackstarfarms.com/inn

The setting is the most impressive feature here: this inn is surrounded by 160 acres of orchards and vineyards with their seasonally changing appearance. The facilities are superb, too. Each contemporary-style room has its own private bath, and some rooms have fireplaces or spa tubs. The inn also features sundecks, a sauna, a bar, and a winery tasting room. (When you visit, start with a bottle of the house wine.) There are many food options, too. Fish boils and harvest dinners are served on select days, or head to the Hearth & Vine Café for either lunch of dinner.

1 Keweenaw Mountain Lodge

14252 US 41, Copper Harbor 49918; (906) 289-4403
keweenawmountainlodge.com

Expect a rustic atmosphere in these log cabins, located at the tip of the remote Keweenaw Peninsula. Enjoy the meals, the setting, and the old-style wooden architecture. On cool evenings (which can happen in any season), there are fireplaces to sit in front of and relax. But it's not just luxury that draws people here—it's the mountainous landscape, the big lake, the adventure, and the remoteness of the area (and just maybe a little golfing at the lodge's 9-hole course).

The Kingsley House Bed & Breakfast

626 W. Main St., Fennville 49408; (866) 561-6425, (269) 561-6425
kingsleyhouse.com

This inn is surrounded by beaches in every direction, small towns that accommodate tourists, and a variety of entertainment options. People are drawn by the lake, the sunsets, the antiques, and the total experience, but here the lodging is not an overlooked part of their stay but rather a comfortable place to relax between events. With a spa service, a concierge, and the option of enjoying Jacuzzis and fireplaces, this bed-and-breakfast offers a perfect place to relax.

13 Lake 'N Pines Lodge

10354 Mud Lake Road, Interlochen 49643; (231) 275-6671
lakenpineslodge.com

This lodge is surrounded by Pere Marquette State Forest and is close to Traverse City. Located on Lake Dubonnet, this is a quiet and peaceful place to stay. The lake offers good fishing, and the forest is the perfect place to walk, bird-watch, or look for flowers. You could spend your entire stay happily just on property, but you can also feel free to use it as your home base from which to explore the local communities, parks, and wineries. With only the lodge and a few homes on the lake, you'll feel as though you have discovered an unknown wilderness that is home to loons, ospreys, and a variety of wildlife. This area is also the home of the Interlochen Center for the Arts (see the Fine Arts chapter, page 41), and catching a concert or performance can be the highlight of any vacation retreat.

14 Laurium Manor Inn

320 Tamarack St., Laurium 49913; (906) 337-2549
laurium.info

Now a National Historic Site, this inn was originally a 45-room mansion built for a copper-mine owner in 1908. All the rooms have a private bath, and most have a whirlpool, fireplace, and private balcony, which certainly meets our definition of a mansion. Just make sure your schedule allows time to explore the tiled porch, the library the den, and the parlor, as well as the rare hand-painted murals, antiques, and furnishings. The breakfast each day is a full buffet. Across the street, Victorian Hall B&B, run in conjunction with the inn, offers more lodging options.

15 Michigan's Little Bavaria

Frankenmuth Chamber of Commerce and Convention & Visitors Bureau, 635 S. Main St., Frankenmuth 48734; (800) 386-8696
frankenmuth.org/summer-getaway-frankenmuth

Frankenmuth is as German as you can get in Michigan—think of a visit here as an international trip without a passport. The shops, the restaurants, and the architecture are designed to transport you to another place, and your only obligation is to relax. When you're here, grab an all-you-can-eat, family-style chicken dinner at either Zehnder's or the Bavarian Inn—two of the most successful restaurants in America—and wash it down with a local beer. Then walk the waterfront and check out the wooden bridge and glockenspiel. If you have kids with you, you might want to also check out the indoor waterpark. This is also a town of festivals (see our listings starting on page 182), so you may want to schedule your visit when a specific event is happening.

6 Portage Point Resort

8567 Portage Point Drive, Onekama 49675; (231) 889-7500
portagepointresort.com

Since 1903, this resort has been emphasizing family vacations. It is located on the inland Portage Lake but is only a short walk from Lake Michigan's sandy beach. With a new marina, this is a welcome location for boaters and fishing. Portage Point offers many activities for children, and adults have a variety of options to enjoy, including golf and a casino. Located on a wooded peninsula, the inn borders both lakes, and an inland channel provides protection and a haven when weather is challenging. Many experienced visitors recommend bringing your own food to grill, so you don't have to leave the comfort of the inn and beach. Consider visiting in winter for a cozy stay that involves some tobogganing and skiing.

Rosemont Inn

83 Lakeshore Drive, Douglas 49406; (269) 857-2637
rosemontinn.com

Enjoy the warmth of a fireplace after a day of exploring the beach in summer or a day skiing the trails in winter. The local art galleries and the scenic views of Lake Michigan are both sources of inspiration, and biking and hiking offer quiet ways to explore the area. The bed-and-breakfast also has an outdoor pool, a coffee and tea bar, and a waterfall meditation garden. Even though there are many activities to occupy your time, consider setting some time aside for quiet contemplation. If that doesn't make you feel pampered enough, you can retire to your four-poster bed for a night of peaceful rest.

Stafford's Bay View Inn

2011 Woodland Ave., Petoskey 49770; (231) 347-2771, (800) 737-1899
thebayviewinn.com

This inn, and especially its outside veranda, offers a lovely view of the lake. This 1886 inn harks back to the romance of historic times and

maintains a lodge just a stone's throw from the mild waves of Little Traverse Bay. It is conveniently located near a bike trail and a wonderful waterfront park, and it's only a short distance from downtown Petoskey. The inn's Roselawn Dining Room is a very popular seasonal dining destination.

19 The Vineyard Inn

1338 N. Pebble Beach Drive, Suttons Bay 49682; (231) 941-7060
vininn.com

Located in the wine country of the Leelanau Peninsula, The Vineyard Inn promotes romantic escapes and boasts 12 beachfront suites. There is an on-site bistro and a tasting room for their very own nearby French Valley Vineyards. The inn's rooms have a European flair, lake views from every suite, pillow-top beds, and modern interiors. Each lakeview suite has a patio or balcony overlooking beautiful Suttons Bay. The inn also offers a limousine coach service to shepherd visitors to the area wineries or take them sightseeing at the dunes and lighthouses.

20 Walloon Lake Inn

4178 West St., Walloon Lake 49796; (231) 535-2999
walloonlakeinn.com

These are Ernest Hemingway's old stomping grounds, and like Hemingway, you might want to enjoy the clear waters and fishing of Walloon Lake. You can do so at the Walloon Lake Inn, but it has more to offer than just excellent lake views—this fine-dining restaurant has earned national acclaim. Originally known as the Fern Cottage, the Walloon Lake Inn is 130 years old and continues to provide quiet country ambiance along with delicious food. Steamboats may not tie up at the dock anymore, but the sense of history is still here.

Copper Harbor, Keweenaw Peninsula

Dow Gardens

FROM THE STATE'S southern border to the northern tip of the Keweenaw Peninsula, Michigan's climate and habitat vary a great deal. The lake effect produced by the Great Lakes affects Michigan's weather patterns and growing seasons, and each Great Lake has a steady temperature that helps hold back the frost. This allows wonderful garden and forest displays to persist from May through October.

GARDENS, FLOWERS, ARBORETUMS & FORESTS

(continued on next page)

rtwick Pines State Park

1 Anna Scripps Whitcomb Conservatory at Belle Isle Conservancy

Belle Isle Park 99 Pleasure Drive, Detroit 48207; (313) 821-9844, (313) 821-5428
belleislepark.org, belleisleconservancy.org

The building for this conservatory, which dates back to 1904, is a historic monument in itself. Yet it isn't just a building; its Victorian design still houses beautiful flora and invites visitors to its warm and humid interior. Palms soar to the glass domes, and flowers and fruits are all around in abundance. If you have only a limited time, concentrate on the orchids, the conservatory's primary claim to fame. In the summer, be sure to stroll the outdoor gardens, too. *Note:* A Michigan Recreation Passport (see page 5) is required for vehicles to enter Belle Isle, the island on which the conservatory and park are located, but pedestrians and cylists may enter free of charge.

The Anna Scripps Conservatory on Belle Island

Cooley Gardens

Capitol Avenue at Main Street, Lansing 48833; (517) 483-4332
michigan.org/property/cooley-gardens

Most arboretums or public gardens are found at the edge of cities or in the suburbs, but the Cooley Gardens are nearly in the center of Lansing, just south of the state capitol and the central business district. It is a beautiful little pocket garden situated on just 1 acre of land. This semiformal garden has a very private feeling to it and seems right out of a romance novel. It can be challenging to find, but the visit is well worth the effort.

Dow Gardens

1809 Eastman Ave., Midland 48640; (800) 362-4874, (989) 631-2677
dowgardens.org

This garden and arboretum was once the personal playground of Herbert Dow of Dow Chemical, but now it is open to the public. The flowers are grouped in such a way that you'll feel like you are making discoveries as you walk through the parkland forest. There are places of seclusion, open grass areas, showy roses and tulips, and seasonal displays. A quiet stream meanders through the gardens and conveys a sense of peace and meditation, while inviting birds to be part of your observations. Metal sculptures enhance the landscape, and a children's garden and organic vegetable display provide other diversions.

Fernwood Botanical Garden and Nature Preserve

13988 Range Line Road, Niles 49120; (269) 695-6491
fernwoodbotanical.org

Situated on the St. Joseph River in southwest Michigan, between Buchanan and Niles, Fernwood comprises 105 acres of gardens and natural areas. Visitors may enjoy woodlands, a prairie, cultivated gardens, an arboretum, springs, ponds, and walking and hiking trails. Other features include a nature center, fern conservatory, art gallery, library, café, and garden and gift shops. The garden features an herb garden, rock garden, boxwood garden, fern and hosta collections, railway garden, children's nature adventure garden, English cottage border, Japanese garden, and more. Fernwood offers something to engage every visitor.

Frederik Meijer Gardens & Sculpture Park

1000 E. Beltline Ave. NE, Grand Rapids 49525; (888) 957-1580, (616) 957-1580
meijergardens.org

The Frederik Meijer Gardens & Sculpture garden is as popular as it is revered. Named one of the top 100 most-popular museums in the US

by Art Newspaper, it spans more than 150 acres and is home to a variety of wonderful gardens. These green spaces range from formal English-style gardens to a sprawling garden built for the younger set and a huge conservatory full of tropical plants. The art on site is as fine as the gardens; there are sculptures by world-famous artists such as Rodin (creator of the famous *The Thinker*) as well as Henry Moore, among many others, and the indoor gallery hosts world-class-level exhibits as well.

6 Hartwick Pines State Park and Logging Museum

4216 Ranger Road, Grayling 49738; (989) 348-2537
tinyurl.com/hartwickpines

This is a garden that nature planted. The site's 49 acres of old-growth pine are the heart of this forest, where you can admire the history and ecology of the white pine. The trees here are 250–400 years old and deserve our respect. After your orientation at the visitor center, you can go to the Hartwick Pines Logging Museum where you can learn about the early days of logging. You'll also want to make sure you stop in at the visitor center to see if you can catch a nature programming event. *Note:* Michigan Recreation Passport required (see page 5 for more information).

7 Hidden Lake Gardens

6214 Monroe Road (M-50), Tipton 49287; (517) 431-2060
canr.msu.edu/hiddenlakegardens

Located in Michigan's Irish Hills, this 755-acre plant bonanza is owned and maintained by Michigan State University. This garden displays plants from a variety of zones, from temperate to tropical. The tropical plants, housed in a dome, include cacao, papaya, coffee and tapioca, while a visit to the cactus dome is an escape to a different environment altogether. Make sure you also stop and see the nationally renowned collections of hostas and rare conifers. Plan to stop at the visitor center for an orientation.

Holland Tulips

Tulip Time Festival Office, 42 W. Eighth St., Holland 49423; (800) 822-2770, (616) 396-4221
tuliptime.com/events, holland.org/events/tulip-festival

Six million tulips bloom each spring throughout Holland, Michigan, and it all started with a Woman's Literary Club meeting in 1929. There, Miss Lida Rogers, a local biology teacher, suggested that Holland adopt the tulip as the city's official flower and celebrate this with a festival. The idea caught on, and in 1928 the city council purchased 100,000 tulip bulbs from the Netherlands to plant in city parks and other areas. In the spring of 1929, thousands of tulips bloomed, and the long history of the annual Tulip Time Festival started. This early-May festival has grown considerably since then, with nine days of fun: parades, entertainment, *klompen* (wooden shoe) dancing, fireworks, and lots of Dutch food, merchandise, and demonstrations. Of course, the number-one attraction is still the tulip itself—and there are literally millions to see across the city. Veldheer's Tulip Farm alone plants approximately 5 million tulips every year. If you want to try planting your own tulips, fall preorders for tulips are taken at various locations.

Kensington Metropark Farm Center

4570 Huron River Parkway, Milford 48380; (810) 227-2757, (248) 684-8632
metroparks.com/kensington-metropark-farm-center

Bringing a sense of farming to urban populations is more important than ever before as more people become distanced from their agricultural roots. The Farm Center is both a walk back in time and a walk into nature. From maple syrup in the spring to pumpkins in the fall, there's always something happening here, and opportunities to participate in the Farm Center abound. The restored barn, the kids' cottage, and the farm animals will charm young ones and parents alike.

Loda Lake Wildflower Sanctuary

Huron-Manistee National Forest Baldwin/White Cloud Ranger District, (231) 745-4631
tinyurl.com/lodalake

Visit Loda Lake in the Huron-Manistee National Forests to see the full splendor of North American wildflowers. Maintained in a unique partnership between the U.S. Forest Service and the Michigan Garden Clubs, this former white pine forest was logged in the 1890s by the railroad; unable to convert it to farmland, landowners were happy to sell it to the national forest during the Depression. Today, you can enjoy more than 400 species in their natural settings. Follow the paths, carry a field guide and a camera (and binoculars because the

birds like this area, too), and explore the diversity that comes with a little elevation change or a different angle of light. Special prizes to be found here include pink lady's slipper, jack-in-the-pulpit, pitcher plant, Indian pipe, swamp milkweed, and wild bergamot. Trail maps are available on-site.

11 Matthaei Botanical Gardens and Nichols Arboretum

Matthaei Botanical Gardens 1800 N. Dixboro Road, Ann Arbor 48105; (734) 647-7600

Nichols Arboretum 1610 Washington Heights, Ann Arbor 48104; (734) 647-8986 lsa.umich.edu/mbg

Matthaei Botanical Gardens is located on Ann Arbor's east side, and Nichols Arboretum is on the University of Michigan Central Campus. Both properties are owned by the University of Michigan. Together, they offer 375 acres of gardens, research areas, and natural preserves. At the botanical gardens you will find highlights that include a large conservatory with tropical, temperate, and arid houses; the Alexandra Hicks Herb Knot Garden, a classic geometrically designed planting; a Gateway Garden, filled with seasonal New World annuals, spring bulbs, and native perennials; a garden of Great Lakes native plants in habitats such as wetland and dunes; a large seasonal outdoor bonsai garden; native prairie and woodland wildflowers; and more. That is a lot to choose from, but you can always get oriented at the visitor center, where they can tell you what's in bloom and where the trails lead. Nichols Arboretum features collections of native and exotic shrubs and trees throughout its 123 acres, including a collection of over 350 varieties of peonies, a wetland boardwalk, a collection of oak openings, and a prairie. Each June, the Arboretum hosts Shakespeare in the Arb, a theater production that moves through the arboretum.

2 Michigan 4-H Children's Garden

1066 Bogue St., East Lansing 48824; (517) 355-5191, ext. 1327
4hgarden.msu.edu

Inside and out, there are garden options to enjoy in every season on the Michigan State University campus. The garden's name is intended to attract children and pique their interest, but it should not put off adults, who are also sure to get great joy from it. This up-to-date effort to interest children in the world of plants moves from Alice in Wonderland to Harry Potter. A winding path of bricks (think Dorothy in *The Wizard of Oz*) moves everyone through the kid-themed conservancy, which will challenge them and engage them to learn.

3 W. J. Beal Botanical Garden

Michigan State University, West Circle Drive, East Lansing 48824; (517) 355-9582
cpp.msu.edu/beal

The oldest university botanical garden in the United States, this garden has more than 5,000 species of plants. Designed to make self-guided hikes easy, the plants are organized thematically: there are groupings based on evolutionary links, economic links, by landscape, and by ecosystem. There are even some invasive plants in the collection, included to help people recognize them and prevent their spread. The gardens have weeds and prized garden varieties, herbs and poisonous plants, fibers and dyes, medicines, and perfumes—and much more than that. For instance, the garden is home to a variety of plants that are threatened, endangered, or rare in Michigan.

4 W. K. Kellogg Experimental Forest

7060 N. 42nd St., Augusta 49012; (269) 731-4597
canr.msu.edu/kelloggforest

There are places you can go in Michigan to see old-grown trees, but the W. K. Kellogg Experimental Forest highlights something else: the reforestation of abandoned agricultural land. This is primarily a research site of Michigan State University, but it is open to the public, and anyone who has an interest in trees in general and forest management will likely enjoy a visit. Since 1932, scientists and arborists here have worked on tree breeding and genetics, planting techniques, and land management. The public can visit to learn tips for managing their own land and gain glimpses of ongoing research. The forest also provides recreation, such as bow hunting, trout fishing, jogging, picnicking, biking, hiking, horseback riding, and cross-country skiing. There are a couple ways to enjoy the area when you visit: you can drive the loop or walk the interpretive trails.

Detroit Beer Company

MICHIGAN IS THE PLACE FOR GOOD TIMES and good beverages. With nearly 400 breweries in the state, we can offer only a sampling here. Your challenge is to try them all! Or if you prefer, just find the places closest to you and have a great time (responsibly, of course). For even more options, see our Festivals listings for "Agriculture/Food & Drink" (page 189) and "Vineyards & Wineries" (page 194).

GOOD SPIRITS & GOOD TIMES

(continued on next page)

There are beer flights aplenty across Michigan.

4 Various locations

1 Arbor Brewing Company

Plymouth Taproom 777 W. Ann Arbor Trail, Plymouth 48104; (734) 233-6201

Corner Brewery 720 Norris St., Ypsilanti 48198; (734) 480-2739
arborbrewing.com

Founded in Ann Arbor as only the fifth brewery in the state, Arbor Brewing Company has now expanded to two locations. While you can get many types of craft beer here, Arbor specializes in sours, and a new monthly program produces original, small-batch beers that are available only for a limited time, so there's always something new for you to try. Both locations also have extensive food menus, so you can bring the whole family.

2 BAD Brewing Company

440 S. Jefferson St., Mason 48854; (517) 676-7664
badbrewing.com

Founded in 2012, BAD Brewing has close to two dozen in-house beers on tap, as well as at least one cider. Enjoy your beer in the pub or head out back to the beer garden, where you might find fun activities such as music and trivia. While you're there, make sure to grab something from the Good Bites food truck (the pan-fried mac and cheese is a local favorite).

3 Batch Brewing Company

1400 Porter St., Detroit 48216
batchbrewingcompany.com

Nanobrewing is the newest phase in the microbrewing industry: small batches, a constantly changing tap, and lots of tastes to explore. But while the beer is delicious and a treat for the taste buds, the food at this nanobrewery is so good that the *Detroit News* did a restaurant review. Among its delicious options is their praline bread pudding. The brewery is also known for starting the Feelgood Tap program, which raises money for nonprofits across the state.

Beer, Wine, and Spirits Trails & Tours

Michigan Breweries & Brewpubs Map brewtrail.com/michigan-breweries

Pure Michigan Wine, Beer, and Spirits Trail Listings michigan.org/wine-beer
-spirit-trails

West Michigan Beer Tours westmichiganbeertours.com

If variety is what you're looking for, you might want to look into one
of the many wine, beer, and spirits trails and tours in Michigan. These
experiences tend to focus on a specific region in Michigan, such as the
Thumb area or Grand Rapids. If you don't see one where you plan on
visiting, you can also plan and create your own tour. Just make sure you
enjoy responsibly if you plan on driving to multiple locations in one day.
Better yet, spend the night at a bed-and-breakfast that's located near a
wine trail—see laketolake.com/experiences/wine-trail for suggestions.

Bell's Eccentric Café

355 E. Kalamazoo Ave., Kalamazoo 49007; (269) 382-2332
bellsbeer.com/eccentric-cafe

Because its beer is distributed in other states, Bell's has established a
reputation and following that make the Eccentric Café a great place
for a beer lover's pilgrimage. Everyone knows that if a beer is good in
a bottle, it's even better on tap—and a sampler is an excellent way to
taste the range of styles. Laid-back and spacious, the restaurant serves
food that matches the quality of the beer. There is also an outside
courtyard where you can enjoy beer and sun. When you're done, visit
their beer store in the corner of the building.

The B.O.B.

20 Monroe Ave. NW, Grand Rapids 49503; (616) 356-2000
thebob.com

The first microbrewery in Grand Rapids, B.O.B. gets its name from its
"big old building," which encompasses 70,000 square feet. B.O.B.'s
Brewery serves its own popular brews, along with burgers and other
pub food. The building itself houses a variety of different events—
everything from billiards and jazz to dance and comedy.

Café d'Mongo's Speakeasy

1439 Griswold St., Detroit 48226; no phone
tinyurl.com/cafedmongos

Known for its Peking duck—actually a recipe handed down by the
owner's great-grandmother from South Carolina—this is a café with
character. Listen to jazz and enjoy the setting while you imagine yourself in a Prohibition-era speakeasy. Café D'Mongo doesn't brew its own

beer, but they are known for creating two regionally popular drinks: if you go, ask for the 1439 (Captain Morgan and Faygo Rock & Rye soda) or the Detroit Brown (Vernors, bitters, and Crown Royal).

8 Detroit Beer Company

1529 Broadway, Detroit 48226; (313) 962-1529
detroitbeerco.com

Located in downtown Detroit, the Detroit Beer Company is close enough to Comerica Park, Ford Field, and the theater district to be included in a nice evening on the town. Its location in the restored Hartz Building is a perfect fit, and when you go inside and see the massive brew tanks, you'll know that you have a lot of flavors to sample. A tasty, well-prepared bar menu accompanies the beers.

9 The Earle

121 W. Washington St., Ann Arbor 48104; (734) 994-0211
theearle.com

Imagine French and Italian country cuisine served to the sound of live music and paired with great wine. For 35 years and counting, The Earle's wine list has been included in *Wine Spectator*'s Best of Award of Excellence list, honoring restaurants around the world with superb wine offerings. This is old-fashioned dining and relaxation at its finest, making The Earle a wonderful place to visit.

10 Fitzgerald's Hotel & Restaurant

5033 Front St., Eagle River 49950; (906) 337-0666
fitzgeralds-mi.com

With this inn and restaurant being so far north, you might be surprised to hear that they specialize in Southern-style barbecue. They also have excellent whiskey and cocktail selections. The restaurant and bar have windows facing Lake Superior, and if you time your visit right, you can watch the sun set as you eat. With fewer than 100 permanent inhabitants, Eagle River can be safely called a quaint coastal town, but with an old lighthouse, a tall waterfall, and an extensive beach, there's a lot to do here.

1 Founders Brewing Company

235 Grandville Ave. SW, Grand Rapids 49503; (616) 776-1195
foundersbrewing.com

Founders is one of the better known breweries in Michigan—and for good reason. They are one of the larger breweries in the country, but their focus has always been on brewing for "renegades and rebels" who want something different from their beer. The KBS (Kentucky Breakfast Stout), All-Day IPA, and Dirty Bastard are some of their more well-known beers, but if you go to the taproom you can sample small-batch styles that aren't sold anywhere else. The original location is in Grand Rapids, but there is a second location in Detroit.

2 Frankenmuth Brewery Company

425 S. Main St., Frankenmuth 48734; (989) 262-8300
frankenmuthbrewery.com

If you want a brewery that's been around for a while, this is the place to go. They began crafting ales and lagers in 1862, which makes them the oldest microbrewery in the country. This city of festivals is a tourist mecca and the place to go for German-style beers, and the Frankenmuth Brewery Company is home to some of the best beer in town. Their lagers and ales have won many awards, so come, taste, and take a tour of the brewery. Frankie's Root Bier is also made here. The patio and outdoor dining along the Cass River will make the experience even more enjoyable.

3 Green Bird Organic Cellars

9825 Engles Road, Northport 49670; (231) 386-5636
greenbirdcellars.com

Advertised as the state's first (and only) certified organic vineyard, orchard, and winery, this 67-acre farm lets you enjoy the flavor of food and wine that have been sustainably grown and harvested. Grapes are the primary crop, and they grow them without artificial pesticides, herbicides, or fertilizers to allow the grapes to get the true flavor of the sun and soil. Visit the tasting room to try their wines and hard ciders, or try a more in-depth experience and take a tour of the farm and orchards. The tour, led by one of the owners, includes a private tasting.

14 Lily's Seafood Grill and Brewery

410 S. Washington Ave., Royal Oak 48067; (248) 591-5459
lilysseafood.com

The Great Lakes State has lots of shoreline but no seashore, but that
is not a problem for seafood lovers at Lily's. Inspired by their Scottish
grandmother, Lily Strange, the founders of this restaurant have made
this the perfect venue for conversation and relaxation with a right-at-
home feeling. The seafood has been a menu staple since 1999, and
handcrafted beers add to the dining pleasure. Even the décor is filled
with shrimp and fish, but don't worry if your companion doesn't
eat seafood; there are a few pork and chicken options, too. For the
under-21 crowd, try the house-made root beer.

15 The Livery

190 Fifth St., Benton Harbor 49022; (269) 925-8760
liverybrew.com

Located in the art district of a quiet beach town, The Livery
serves great beers and excellent foods that keep bringing people
back for more. Live and lively music adds a festive mood to the
more than 100-year-old former horse stable. If the music and
sound level are not to your liking, the dog-friendly outdoor beer
garden is a pleasant escape.

16 Michigan House Cafe and Red Jacket Brewing Company

300 Sixth St., Calumet 49913; (906) 337-1910
michiganhousecafe.com

Thanks to its history as a mining town, Calumet has a history of
beer drinking, so it's only appropriate that the town now has its
own brewpub for visitors and locals alike. Located downtown and
only two blocks from ski and snowmobile trails, the pub is ready to
refresh you. This is a full-service restaurant in addition to the vintage
pub, and there is lodging on the second floor. The pub is home to
Red Jacket Brewing Company, which follows the tradition of Bosch
Brewing, and has been open since 1905. When you visit, you'll want

to take in the century-old stained glass windows and bar mural. The pub's Oatmeal Espress stout gets lots of rave reviews, and on many Fridays there's live music.

17 Ore Dock Brewing Company

114 Spring St., Marquette 49855; (906) 228-8888
ore-dock.com

This brewery was born out of a desire to create a brewery whose flavors and atmosphere were reflective of Michigan's Upper Peninsula. Water from Lake Superior, barley from England and France—even the ingredients capture the unique "little bit of everything" nature of the peninsula. Tradition also plays a role. The brewery, which is in a building more than 150 years old, strives to live up to centuries of standards that have developed in beer craft. Ore Dock is also very involved in the local community; for example, they sponsor the annual Festival of the Angry Bear (see page 190). Check the website before you go to see what special events they might be having.

8 Rochester Mills Beer Co.

400 Water St., Rochester 49307; (248) 650-5080
beercos.com

This brewery is located in the building of the historic Western Knitting Mill, and they've done an excellent job of restoring many of the original architectural features. With good food, a neat building, and excellent beer, there is nothing lacking here, so visit and enjoy the pool tables and the outdoor patio. Live music plays in the evening from Thursday through Sunday.

9 Short's Brewing Company

121 N. Bridge St., Bellaire 49615; (231) 498-2300
shortsbrewing.com

Short's wants to create the "best beer on earth," and their strategy is to do so while maintaining the milieu of a small, localized brewery: creativity, excellent customer service, and a mom-and-pop feel. This is how they've been able to grow from needing to hand-label the beers on the first production shipment to being one of the most well-known breweries in Michigan. While you're here, be sure to try their pizza—the dough is made extra flavorful by infusing it with their own beer.

Fort Mackinac

FROM COLONIAL FORTS AND SITES from the War of 1812 to the advent of shipping on the Great Lakes and the rise of Motor City, Michigan has played a unique role in the events that shaped the nation. You can explore some of this legacy at these sites. If you visit all of them, give yourself a passing grade in Michigan history!

MICHIGAN HISTORY

(continued on next page)

111

otswold cottage farmhouse, Greenfield Village

1 Charles H. Wright Museum of African American History

315 E. Warren Ave., Detroit 48201; (313) 494-5800
thewright.org

When Detroit obstetrician Charles Wright opened this museum, the largest museum dedicated to the history and culture of African Americans, he did so with this motto: "And Still We Rise: Our Journey Through African American History and Culture." This museum is both inspiring and challenging. It is home to a slave gallery and one of the most emotional museum walks you'll find anywhere. It also celebrates the impact many great African American minds have had in science, education, religion, and politics. To get the full impact of this experience, allow yourself time to watch and listen to the many videos that are incorporated into the exhibits. This is not a museum that can be explored quickly. Treat yourself to a study of a history that has gone untold for too long.

2 Colonial Michilimackinac

102 W. Straits Ave., Mackinaw City 49701; (231) 436-4100,
(906) 847-3328 (summer only)
mackinacparks.com/colonial-michilimackinac

Located on the Straits of Mackinac near the historic lighthouse museum and the impressive Mackinac Bridge, this reconstructed fort tells a tale of intrigue and adventure. Travel back to the 1770s and learn about muskets and life on the frontier, when French *voyageurs* and American Indians shared the site with British soldiers. Today, costumed interpreters and historical demonstrations make this a lively place. You can climb to the top of the walls and take in the scenery from all directions. There are also special events that can really enhance your visit, such as Fort Fright or special themed weekends. But if you can't make the events, don't worry—every day is filled with fun. There are historical baseball games, firing demonstrations, ongoing archaeological digs, dances, music, crafts, and storytelling. Check the website for an event schedule.

3 Fayette Historic Townsite

4785 II Road, Garden 49835; (906) 644-2603
michigan.gov/fayettetownsite

Be careful when you visit the park, as Snail Shell Harbor and Big Bay de Noc are stunning enough to distract you from this wonderful living museum of a village. The village was the site of a manufacturer of pig iron ingots for 24 years; the iron would be shipped south, where much of it was used in steel railroad construction. Now that story is told in the exhibits within the historic buildings, as well as at the visitor center. Guided and self-guided tours bring the village to life, from the blast furnace to the town hall. Following the trails allows you to explore the beautiful setting. You may have a tough time reconciling the idyllic view and setting of today with the smoky, dirty-smelting operation that once operated here. *Note:* Michigan Recreation Passport required (see page 5).

Fort Mackinac

7127 Huron Road, Mackinac Island 49757; (231) 436-4100
mackinacparks.com/parks-and-attractions/fort-mackinac

Mackinac Island is home to a state park and a community that boasts the oldest building in Michigan. On an island that is historical in every sense of the word, it's hard to focus on just one area, but Fort Mackinac is really the centerpiece of this place. Once you are inside the stone walls, you'll be awash in history. There are costumed interpreters, and special events that place you in the middle of the War of 1812. You might even hear a cannon blast. If talk of war isn't your thing, there is a Tea Room for civilized reflection and one of the island's best views of the harbor. How significant is this historic site? In 1875 it was declared the second national park in the United States; only Yellowstone preceded it. Today, Fort Mackinac is managed as a Michigan state park; check the website for admission and ticket information.

Fort St. Joseph Archaeological Site and Museum

508 E. Main St., Niles 49120 (museum); (269) 845-4054, ext. 2010
nilesmi.org/departments_and_divisions/niles_history_center, wmich.edu/fortstjoseph/outreach

Usually an archaeological project wouldn't be something to consider for a day trip, and while you might not get to pick up a trowel and excavate yourself, one of the goals of this project is to help the general public better understand and experience archaeology. Fort St. Joseph was built in 1691 and remained in use for 90 years, making it one of the oldest forts on the continent. Now it is an archaeological project

that has given real vitality and excitement to the Niles History Center's Fort St. Joseph Museum. This site, often covered by water from the river, is part of the museum's Archaeology Open House, which features costumed reenactors and lots of events for the family; call or check the website for dates and times. The museum itself, which operates in an old carriage house, focuses on the story of Niles from the modern day back to prehistoric times.

6 Freedom Trail (Underground Railroad)

Journey to Freedom: Underground Railroad Bus Tours Presented by the African American Historical and Cultural Museum of Washtenaw County; tours leave from Washtenaw Community College, 4800 E. Huron River Drive, Ann Arbor 48105; (734) 819-8182

Underground Railroad Reading Station Tours Second Baptist Church of Detroit, 441 Monroe St., Detroit 48226; (313) 961-0920

Underground Railroad Society of Cass County Driving Tour Vandalia aachm.org/events-exhibits, ugrrbookstore.com/tours.html, urscc.org/ugrr-site -driving-tour.html

Some stories cannot be captured in a single exhibit or a video. Instead, you need a personal connection, and it takes some effort to begin to comprehend the full extent of the story.

This is especially true of the Freedom Trail, better known as the Underground Railroad. This highly charged and emotional story is, of course, about fleeing slavery in the early 19th century: imagine traveling by night and hiding in basements and outbuildings while trying to outrun and outsmart men with guns, whips, and dogs. This is a terrible part of the larger story of the United States, but one that must be told. The stories of those courageous slaves who fled—and the tales of the people who sheltered them—are too often forgotten.

It's difficult to trace the physical route of the Freedom Trail/Underground Railroad, which wasn't a literal trail or railroad but an amorphous network of escape routes. African-Americans were the driving force behind this dangerous (and at the time, unpopular) endeavor, though there was some white Quaker support. Within Michigan, a number of related historical sites no longer exist, having been torn down long ago, and visiting the existing sites is largely a matter of planning your own itinerary. A few notable guided and self-guided tours are available, however.

The African American Historical and Cultural Museum of Washtenaw County leads guided Underground Railroad bus tours of sites in Ann Arbor, Pittsfield Township, and Ypsilanti. In a number of Michigan cities; tours are led by a museum interpreter and affiliated with the National Park Service's National Underground Railroad Network to Freedom (nps.gov/ugrr)—a database of more than 650 sites, programs, and facilities around the U.S. that have a connection to the Underground Railroad—the tours are limited to 30 guests and visit historically significant cemeteries, homes, buildings, and other sites.

The Underground Railroad Reading Station, an independent bookstore and gift shop located at Second Baptist Church of Detroit, leads tours of the church (note: not offered at the time of this writing but expected to resume in late 2021 or 2022). First organized in 1836, Second Baptist is the oldest Black church in the Midwest and was a local stop on the Underground Railroad; the current church building dates from 1914. A TripAdvisor reviewer calls the tour "a hidden gem" of Detroit.

The Underground Railroad Society of Cass County offers a self-guided driving tour, complete with printable maps, highlighting 20 sites within 4 miles of Vandalia, in southwest Michigan. See the website for details.

(For a list of Freedom Trail/Underground Railroad sites in Michigan, go to tinyurl.com/exploreugrrsites and enter "Michigan" in the search box.)

7 Gerald R. Ford Presidential Library & Museum

Library 1000 Beal Ave., Ann Arbor 48109; (734) 205-0555

Museum 303 Pearl St. NW, Grand Rapids 49504; (616) 254-0400
fordlibrarymuseum.gov

Ascending to the presidency after the resignations of Spiro Agnew and Richard M. Nixon, Gerald Ford entered the White House at an incredibly trying time in U.S. history. You can see this history up-close at the Gerald R. Ford Presidential Museum in Grand Rapids or at the Gerald R. Ford Library in Ann Arbor. While the library is dedicated to research, the museum tells a story of the uneasy days when a vice president and then a president resigned, requiring replacements according to the rules of presidential succession in the Constitution.

The sites are home to a number of temporary exhibits, but a permanent exhibit collection dedicated to the lives of President Ford and First Lady Betty Ford is always present. In the permanent collection you will also learn about the 1970s, a turbulent era when the Constitution was being tested; plus, you'll see images of the White House and learn about the important international affairs during President Ford's term. This is a compelling story, and one that is well told.

8 Greenfield Village

The Henry Ford 20900 Oakwood Blvd., Dearborn 48124; (313) 982-6001
thehenryford.org/visit/greenfield-village

Pair this village experience with the Henry Ford Museum (see page 74), and you'll have at least one full day of learning and fun. As this site demonstrates, history is anything but boring. With special events, such as Holiday Nights and a number of car shows, the village is constantly changing and worth revisiting. Even so, the basic experience is so well done that it stands alone without the extras. From the Model T rides and historic horse-drawn carriages to sites like Thomas Edison's laboratory, Lincoln's courthouse, and the Wright Brothers' cycle shop, the village brings history to life. This is a complete village—not just isolated buildings—and the costumed actors here help make the time travel even more real.

9 Keweenaw National Historical Park

25970 Red Jacket Road, Calumet 49913; (906) 483-3176
nps.gov/kewe

Copper mining is the focus of this national historical park, but there's a lot more to see here, including lighthouses, nature preserves, and charming communities, all of which are intertwined in a driving tour. The park offers excellent exhibits and stories at its Calumet Visitor Center, which also serves as a tourist information center linking the mining tours, museums, and historic sites so you can maximize your time and exploration. If you drop in at the visitor center in Calumet, be sure to also check out the full town, which has museums and monuments honoring the town's mining past. The most dramatic story of Calumet is the Strike of 1913 (and the subsequent Italian Hall massacre), which was eventually the basis for a Woody Guthrie song

10 Michigan Heroes Museum

1250 Weiss St., Frankenmuth 48734; (989) 652-8005
facebook.com/miheroes

Honoring the efforts and stories of 16 of Michigan's astronauts, 31 of its Medal of Honor recipients, and a number of its governors who served in the military, this museum tells a global story through the tales of individuals from Michigan. Everything from the Spanish-American War to the War on Terror is included here, and because the museum is located in popular Frankenmuth, it's easy to add to many different day-travel adventures.

11 Michigan History Museum

702 W. Kalamazoo St., Lansing 48915; (517) 373-1359
michigan.gov/museum

When it comes to teaching kids about history, interactive exhibits are key, and this museum has exhibits that will draw in visitors of any age. As one commented, "I didn't know Michigan had so much history." Well, it does, and the five levels of the Michigan Historical Center cover all of it, from prehistory to the present day. At the beginning of the museum, there is a three-story relief map of Michigan, and as a map person, I found it almost hard to leave. Even so, there's much more to see—you'll want to see how the museum re-created a copper mine from the U.P. and depicts the stories of the lower peninsula.

2 Michigan Military Technical & Historical Society

16600 Stephens Road, Eastpointe 48021; (586) 872-2581
mimths.org

A combination of models, replicas, artifacts, and exhibits honors the stories of Michigan natives who have served with distinction in defense of our nation. The museum covers the period from World War I through the present day and connects visitor with the heroes who have fought and sacrificed for our nation. Check the website for information on lecture series, reenactments, and other special events.

3 Museum of Ojibwa Culture

500 N. State St., St. Ignace 49781; (906) 643-9161
museumofojibwaculture.net

This museum showcases Ojibwa history in the Great Lakes region, particularly the complicated relationship between the French and the native Ojibwa, Ottawa, and Huron peoples, who all met near the Straits of Mackinac in the 1600s. Exhibits in the museum feature glimpses into Ojibwa family networks, Huron longhouses, and native technologies. The museum's most compelling exhibit recounts the silencing and abuse that occurred at the Holy Childhood of Jesus Indian School in the 1800s. There is more to the museum than exhibits, however; it provides visitors with free guided walking tours of the area, hosts a number of cultural events, and provides a place for native artists to share their work.

14 Port Huron Museums

1115 Sixth St., Port Huron 48060; (810) 982-0891
phmuseum.org

The Port Huron Museums consist of five different sites. The Thomas Edison Depot (built in 1858) is the actual structure where Edison worked from 1859 to 1863, peddling his self-published newspaper to passengers riding the train between Port Huron and Detroit. Step inside the depot, and discover his chemistry lab and printing shop. The Fort Gratiot Light is only a few steps away—tour the oldest lighthouse tower in Michigan, built in 1829, located on 5 acres and adjacent to Lake Huron. Just a short distance farther is the historic *Huron* Lightship, which was built in 1920 and became a National Historic Landmark in 1989. (Retired in 1970, the *Huron* was the last floating lighthouse on the Great Lakes.) The Carnegie Center is the complex's main museum, built in 1904 as a public library funded by Andrew Carnegie. Finally, the Fort Gratiot Hospital was built as a military medical facility in 1829, converted to two private homes in 1879, then acquired by the museum and restored as a single building in the early 2000s.

15 River Raisin National Battlefield Park & Visitor Center

333 N. Dixie Highway, Monroe 48162; (734) 243-7136
nps.gov/rira, riverraisinbattlefield.org

This is one of the newest additions to the National Park System's battlefield collection. Most of us do not know much about the War of 1812, but the battles fought at the River Raisin and the River Raisin Massacre were significant ones. Out of the 400 U.S. Regulars who fought on the right flank on January 22, 1813, only 33 were not killed or captured. The next day, the wounded American soldiers were attacked, and dozens more died in a massacre or were taken captive. The Battlefield and Visitor Center have a diorama and other exhibits that help describe both the battle and the context of the war. The 14-minute fiber optic map is the highlight of the interpretive presentations, but you need to go and see just for yourself how this high-tech demonstration tells the story.

16 Sanilac Petroglyphs Historic State Park

8251 Germania Road, Cass City 48726; (989) 856-4411
tinyurl.com/saniacphsp, michigan.gov/sanilacpetroglyphs

Sanilac Petroglyphs Historic State Park has the Lower Peninsula's only known ancient rock carvings, or petroglyphs. (A petroglyph is carved into rock—a pictograph is *painted on* rock.) A 1-mile hiking trail allows access to the carvings, which in the Ojibwe language are called *Ezhibiigaadek Asin,* which roughly translates to "written on stone." These carvings are somewhere between 600 and 1,000 years old and are subject to erosion because the rock is soft. The website describes the designs as "swirls, lines, handprints, flying birds, and bow-wielding men." The park, which is co-managed by the state and the Saginaw Chippewa Indian Tribe, offers guided tours and interpretation in the summer months. *Note:* Michigan Recreation Passport required (see page 5).

7 Ziibiwing Center of Anishinabe Culture & Lifeways

6650 E. Broadway St., Mt. Pleasant 48858; (989) 775-4750
sagchip.org/ziibiwing

Three bands of the Saginaw Chippewa Indian Tribe of Michigan have combined to build this museum, which serves as a gathering point and a way to reclaim their heritage and history. It is open to everyone and is an important part of the story of the land we now call Michigan. These exhibits share their beliefs and stories in an effort to educate band members and visitors alike. It is important to show respect as you observe and learn about the culture and history of the area, as well as the hardships endured by the Ojibwa people.

The rugged beauty of Isle Royale National Park

THE COOL WATERS of the Great Lakes surround some of the most interesting islands in the world. Here you can find everything from a 19th-century getaway to remote wilderness landscapes. If you don't have a boat, that's no problem; there are numerous ferries to some of the more popular locations and bridges to others. If you have a boat, even more remote adventures await. But no matter what, don't put off your island-hopping, as there's simply so much to see.

ISLAND DESTINATIONS

1 Beaver Islands

Beaver Island Chamber of Commerce, PO Box 5, Beaver Island 49782;
(231) 448-2505
beaverisland.org

Claimed to be the most remote of the Great Lakes' inhabited islands, Beaver Island, part of the Beaver Island Archipelago, is the largest island in Lake Michigan. Home to a year-round population of 600 people of mostly Irish descent, the island has a strange history. In 1850, a Mormon man named James Strang declared the island a monarchy and named himself king. After his assassination, a wave of Irish immigrants moved to the island, which they called "America's Emerald Isle." Today, the island is a destination for those seeking the quiet of nature, and many people like to tour the full archipelago by boat or plane. Located 32 miles from Charlevoix, you can get to the main island by Island Airways and Fresh Air Aviation or via the Beaver Island Boat Company (which offers auto ferry service from Charlevoix). Driving, biking, and hiking are the best ways to explore the island.

2 Drummond Island

Drummond Island Tourism Association 34974 S. Townline Road (PO Box 200), Drummond Island 49726; (906) 493-5245
drummondisland.com, visitdrummondisland.com

Located only 1 mile from the eastern tip of Michigan's Upper Peninsula, a quick glance at the map might lead you to think this is just part of the peninsula, but once you discover the truth, you'll be treated to a real island experience. Visitors can reach the island by plane or boat and can bring along their car or snowmobile thanks to the auto ferry from DeTour Village. Once you're on the island, there's much to do, including bird-watching or fishing in the inland lakes. There is also a wonderful lighthouse to explore here, the DeTour Reef Light. A state forest campground and the Drummond Island Township Park provide primitive camping facilities. Boat owners will also find a full-service marina. If you don't have your own boat, there are charter services for touring and fishing. You will also find a few stores for supplies, a golf course, and snowmobile rentals in the winter.

Grand Island National Recreation Area

Munising Ranger District 400 E. Munising Ave., Munising 49862; (906) 387-2512, (906) 387-3700

Grand Island Ferry Service N8016 Grand Island Landing Road, Munising 49862; (906) 387-2600
grandislandup.com

How can such a large island be a hidden gem? This island features 300-foot cliffs, forest, inland lakes, and even an abandoned lighthouse—plus the island is easy to access by ferry service. And yet the island sees fewer than 10,000 visitors each year. Once there, you can explore the island by trail or bike, and with a boat you can explore the wild and dramatic shoreline. There are also rustic cabins, campsites, bus tours, and fishing opportunities. Many people rent (or bring) their own bike or kayak to explore the island. Just be prepared, because this is a wilderness island without support facilities.

Isle Royale National Park

Houghton Visitor Center 800 E. Lakeshore Drive, Houghton 49931; (906) 482-0984
For directions to the island, see nps.gov/isro/planyourvisit/directions.htm.

This is wilderness at its finest and most isolated. Getting to the island is an adventure all its own, either by multihour boat ride or on a float plane. The second-largest Great Lakes island and the largest in Lake Superior, Isle Royale is actually only one of 450 islands in the archipelago. It is approximately 45 miles long and 8.5 miles across and contains roughly 165 miles of trails. Most people who visit the island come for a day trip or camp in the wilderness, though there are also facilities at Rock Harbor Lodge. While on the island, you can enjoy ranger presentations, join tours to Edisen Fishery, go on a Mooswatch Expedition, take a guided tour to Passage Island Lighthouse, hike to Minong Mine, or enjoy the sunset at Raspberry Island.

Les Cheneaux Islands

Les Cheneaux Islands Area Tourist Association 680 W. M-134, Cedarville 49719; (888) 364-7526
lescheneaux.net

Mackinac Island is not the only island in the Straits of Mackinac. Thirty-six islands are found in the shadow of the famous island, and, replete with channels and bays, they deserve much more attention than they receive. Roughly translated, *Les Cheneaux* means "the channels" in French, and that describes the sheltered waters that await recreational boaters. Here visitors can find giant forests, miles of trails, and sheltered marinas that serve as the perfect places to begin your fishing expeditions and exploration of Lake Huron. None of the islands are

developed; many are not even recommended destinations and some areas are designated as nature preserves, but sailing and kayaking along these islands remain inspiring experiences. Not to be outdone by the wilds, the communities on the mainland closest to the islands also provide entertainment, such as the Antique Wooden Boat Show at Hessel and the Great Lakes Boat Building School at Cedarville.

6 Mackinac Island

Mackinac Island Tourism Bureau 7274 Main St., Mackinac Island 49757;
(906) 847-3783
mackinacisland.org, mackinacparks.com

There are many reasons Mackinac Island is the most famous island in the Great Lakes. Located near the strait that separates Lakes Huron and Michigan, this island is a veritable time capsule that continues to provide memorable experiences for all ages. Cars are banned on the island, so travel is limited to bikes, horse and buggy, and walking, so the pace is nice and slow for everyone. With great restaurants and lodges, this could easily be made into more than a day trip, but a one-day trip is possible. However, if you're making it a one-day trip, make sure to focus your visit, as there is simply too much to do here. The following activities are especially popular:

• Exploring Fort Mackinac

• Visiting the Original Mackinac Island Butterfly House

• Trying world-famous Mackinac Island fudge

• Touring the historic Grand Hotel

• Riding a bicycle around the island or mountain biking off-road

• Visiting the Mackinac Art Museum

• Taking a carriage tour of the island

• Visiting Arch Rock and Skull Cave

7 Neebish Island

Ferry service East Neebish Island Ferry Road, about 0.2 mile north of South Scenic Drive, Barbeau 49710; (906) 632-2898
michigan.org/city/neebish-island

Located in the Saint Marys River, which connects Lake Superior and Lake Huron, this wilderness island is actually composed of Big Neebish and Little Neebish Islands. While there are year-round residents on the island, seasonal visitors come each year for camping, fishing, and exploring. The large freighters that pass on each side of the island add an unusual element for visitors to enjoy. Access to the island is by ferry from Barbeau year-round, except for when the river is frozen.

North and South Manitou Islands

Sleeping Bear Dunes National Lakeshore Philip A. Hart Visitor Center, 9922 Front St., Empire 49630; (231) 326-4700
lelandmi.com/things-to-do/manitou-islands.html, nps.gov/slbe/planyourvisit
/northmanitouisland.htm, nps.gov/slbe/planyourvisit/southmanitouisland.htm

Ferry service Fishtown Dock, Leland 49654; (231) 256-9061, manitoutransit.com

With a magnificent shoreline and giant sand dunes to grab your attention at Sleeping Bear Dunes National Lakeshore, you can be forgiven for not thinking of islands when you plan your trip here. Nevertheless, the lakeshore includes two magnificent islands, and both are worthy of a visit. North Manitou is managed as a wilderness and a "cultural landscape" except for a the area around a small historic village. South Manitou is also largely uninhabited, and favorite activities of visitors to the island include visiting the lighthouse or taking one of the guided tours. Ancient white cedars are some of the most significant plants on the islands, and the surrounding waters include numerous shipwrecks. If you pack a lunch, you can take the ferry for a one-day visit, but an overnight stay is a welcome way to experience both islands. No services are available.

Lighthouse Museum near the Mackinac Bridge

OVER ITS HISTORY, Michigan has had more than 150 lighthouses—more than any other state. Lighthouses may no longer be staffed by lighthouse keepers, but they have lost none of their charm, and they still serve as beacons for ships and tourists alike.

LIGHTHOUSES

(continued on next page)

The Crisp Point Lighthouse on Lake Superior

1 40 Mile Point Lighthouse

40 Mile Point Lighthouse Park, 7323 US 23 N., Rogers City 49779; (989) 734-4907
fortymilepointlighthouse.org

This lighthouse, built in 1896, is 40 miles southeast of Mackinac
Point and 40 miles northwest of Thunder Bay, so the name is logical
if you are navigating the lake. When you visit, take a look around
the lighthouse and enjoy its fabulous swath of beach. Unlike most
lighthouses, it isn't located near a point or a stream: 40 Mile Light
was placed here to fill a void between lighthouses and to make sure
navigators could see a lighthouse on their entire journey along this
shore. Even so, the Great Lakes can sometimes be dangerous. On
October 19, 1905, the *Joseph S. Fay* grounded on a sandbar in heavy
seas. Twelve men made it to safety, but the first mate was lost. On
that day a total of 27 wooden vessels went down in the Great Lakes.
The remains of 150 feet of the *Fay*'s wooden hull still rest on the
beach, 200 feet west of the lighthouse.

2 Au Sable Light Station, Pictured Rocks National Lakeshore

Just north of H-58 and east of Hurricane River Campground, Grand Marais 49839;
(906) 494-2660 (summer only), (906) 387-3700
nps.gov/piro/historyculture/ausablelightstation.htm

Pictured Rocks National Lakeshore appears in many sections of this
book. There are many options for a day trip there, one of which is
the Au Sable Light Station. Completed in 1874, this tall, white tower
rises high above the lake and sits amid a complex of buildings. The
3-mile round-trip walk to Au Sable Light Station from the nearest
parking lot is a very pleasant hike, both on the old roadbed and
along the shore. From the shore you can see portions of old shipwrecks, reminders of why the lighthouse was built. When you visit,
take a tour guided by a park ranger to maximize your experience.
Tours available Wednesday through Sunday in the summer.

3 Big Sable Point Lighthouse

5611 N. Lighthouse, Ludington 49431; (231) 845-7417, (231) 843-2423
splka.org/big.html

Big Sable Point Lighthouse, which began operation in 1867, has a black-and-white tower with a 130-step stairway that winds up to the Fresnel lens. You can also explore the gift shop, which was once the old keeper's quarters. A group of volunteers dedicated to the legacy of lighthouses leads guided tours of the lighthouse and shares its stories. As part of a state park full of beaches and dunes, the lighthouse tour can be combined with many activities and could be incorporated into a walking or biking adventure. Seasonal event information can be found on the website.

4 Crisp Point Lighthouse

1944 County Highway 412, Newberry 49868; (906) 658-3600
crisppointlighthouse.org, exploringthenorth.com/crisp/point.html

Crisp Point Light, located in the northeast corner of Luce County, is a highlight on Lake Superior. It has the classic form we all associate with lighthouses but it was also designated by the U.S. Government as a Life Saving Station. This meant that the keeper of the lighthouse did more than keep the light shining; the job entailed braving the treacherous waters in all weather to save as many lives as possible when a ship wrecked or was in distress. Crisp Point Lighthouse became operational on May 5, 1904, and it was then situated on a point, which since has disappeared. In 1965, the Coast Guard destroyed the support structures around the light, and it was in 1992 that the Crisp Point Light Historical Society was formed to preserve the light. Now the lighthouse stands on a long length of sand beach, a beacon to hikers and boaters and a destination for lighthouse lovers.

Eagle Harbor Lighthouse Complex and Museum

670 Lighthouse Road, Eagle Harbor 49950
exploringthenorth.com/eagleharbor/eagleharbor.html

Built in 1851, the red brick Eagle Harbor Lighthouse Complex is designated a Heritage Site of Keweenaw National Historical Park. As copper mining on the peninsula increased, more ships came to the rocky and dangerous Eagle Harbor, so the octagonal light was built to guide the ships past the natural reefs and toward the mines. There's more than just the lighthouse at this location, however; make sure you also check out the restored Life Saving Station, the Keweenaw History Museum, the Maritime Museum, and the Commercial Fishing Museum.

6 | Fort Gratiot Lighthouse

2802 Omar St., Port Huron 48060; (810) 216-6923
phmuseum.org/fort-gratiot-lighthouse

Michigan's shores are dotted with lighthouses, and Fort Gratiot is the oldest in the state and the second oldest on the Great Lakes. The fort was established in 1814, and the first light was built in 1825, but its location and poor design caused it to collapse a few years later. A new site was chosen in 1829 to build the new structure, and an addition was added in the 1860s to bring it to its present height. The still-functioning lighthouse tower is open for observing the lakeshore (closed-toe shoes are required to climb), and a nearby museum provides history of the site.

7 | Grand Traverse Lighthouse

15500 N. Lighthouse Point Road, Northport 49670; (231) 386-7195
grandtraverselighthouse.com

At the tip of Leelanau Peninsula, the Grand Traverse Lighthouse (built in 1852) is a great addition to your wine-tasting adventures on the Leelanau Peninsula, which is home to more than 20 wineries. The lighthouse itself marks the beginning of Grand Traverse Bay. When it comes to its name, you might encounter a bit of confusion, as locals might call this Cat's Head Light or Northport Light. Whatever you call it, it's had an interesting history, including raids from Mormon "pirates" on Beaver Island. Like many of Michigan's lighthouses, the original structure no longer stands, though when it was active it was constantly upgraded to provide the most effective service. Now the lighthouse is available for tours, and if you bring kids along, you can have them participate in the Lighthouse Treasure Hunt.

8 Old Mackinac Point Lighthouse Museum

526 N. Huron Ave., Mackinaw City 49701; (231) 436 4100
mackinacparks.com/old-mackinac-point-lighthouse

Looking like a sturdy house as much as a lighthouse, this museum is on the shore next to the Mackinac Bridge and is part of the Mackinac State Historic Parks complex. Located at the point where Lakes Michigan and Huron meet, this lighthouse occupied an important location during the early days of shipping. Here you will find keeper quarters that have been restored to a 1910 appearance, the Straits of Mackinac Shipwreck Museum, and an exhibit on optics and sounds of lighthouses. As nice as the inside is, the view from the top is probably the most impressive part of the lighthouse, and it's definitely worth stopping to check out. The light operated from 1890 to 1958.

9 Marquette Harbor Lighthouse and Maritime Museum

300 N. Lakeshore Blvd., Marquette 49855; (906) 226-2006
mqtmaritimemuseum.com

This square red lighthouse is the signature building of Marquette Harbor. Weather permitting, you may be able to take a guided tour of the structure. The Maritime Museum, housed in a classic sandstone building—Old City Waterworks—is a collection of artifacts and stories about local lighthouses, Fresnel lenses, shipwrecks, and lighthouse keepers. In this small hidden gem, there are also stories about American Indians, fishermen, and commercial shipping. The museum sits beside an active Coast Guard station, a reminder of the perils of sailing the Great Lakes.

0 New and Old Presque Isle Lighthouses

New Presque Isle Lighthouse 4500 E. Grand Lake Road, Presque Isle 49777

Old Presque Isle Lighthouse 5295 E. Grand Lake Road, Presque Isle 49777
(989) 787-0814 (year-round), (989) 595-9917 (May–October)
presqueislelighthouses.org

If you're keeping track of all the lighthouses you see, you can add two to your list on this one trip. The old lighthouse dates back to 1840 and is rumored to be haunted. The newer lighthouse, Presque Isle Light Station, was built in 1870, is the tallest tower on the Great Lakes that is open to the public and the view is great, but so is the sensation of being on the narrow walkway outside the light. You should also stop and see the 1905 keeper's house, which is now a museum, and the 1870 Harbor Range Light, which honors women lighthouse keepers. Bring a picnic and make an afternoon of it.

11 Point Betsie Lighthouse

3701 Point Betsie Road, Frankfort 49635; (231) 352-7644
pointbetsie.org

All the Great Lakes have lighthouses along their shorelines, and we are fortunate they were not mass-produced in one style. It is the variations that give them so much charm and enhance the landscape. Located on the southern entrance to Manitou Passage, the Point Betsie Lighthouse (active 1857–1937) is just south of Sleeping Bear Dunes National Lakeshore and a nice addition to other adventures in the area. At this lighthouse you'll find a restored lighthouse keeper residence, an exhibit on the ecosystem of the local dunes, and the Boathouse Museum.

12 Point Iroquois Lighthouse

12942 W. Lakeshore Drive, Brimley 49715; (906) 437-5272
saultstemarie.com/attractions/point-iroquois-lighthouse

Ships traveling from Whitefish Point to into the St. Marys River and the Soo Locks sail through one of the most hazardous areas of Lake Superior. The narrowing of the lake at the mouth of the river can create turbulent conditions, and the high volume of traffic only complicates things. Point Iroquois Lighthouse was constructed to help ships navigate this area. The lighthouse and tower are in excellent shape and open for tours. The name of the lighthouse and the point comes from a battle fought in 1662 in which the resident Ojibwa were able to defeat the Iroquois. The area around the lighthouse is sheltered and provides access to a beautiful and peaceful beach, with boardwalks through the sensitive dune area.

13 Pointe aux Barques Lighthouse

7320 Lighthouse Road, Port Hope 48468; (586) 243-1838
pointeauxbarqueslighthouse.org

The original Pointe aux Barques Lighthouse was built using local stone and rock. By 1857, the tower had deteriorated so badly due to weather and fire that it was in desperate need of replacement. The new keeper's house with an attached 89-foot tower was completed the same year, and the beacon has been in continuous operation since that date. The Life Saving Station opened in 1875 (the first one on the Great Lakes) and operated until 1937. The crews at this station have been credited with more than 200 rescues in the surrounding area. The keeper's home has become a free museum filled with lighthouse, Great Lakes, and Huron County history.

14 Sturgeon Point Lighthouse

6071 E. Point Road, Harrisville 48740; (989) 724-6297, (989) 724-6153
alconahistoricalsociety.com/index.php/admission,
tinyurl.com/sturgeonpointstatepark

Protecting ships from a shallow reef in Lake Huron, Sturgeon Point Lighthouse has been in continuous operation since 1870 and is used by recreational as well as commercial vessels. Serious lighthouse observers will recognize this as a Cape Cod–style lighthouse, just one example of the many lighthouse styles found in the state. Volunteers have restored the keeper's house and turned it into a museum. If you look just offshore as you admire the lighthouse, you can see the reason the lighthouse was built: the reef just below the surface. Just to the north is an area known as Sanctuary Bay, a place of safety for ships trying to get to calmer waters. This light is within Sturgeon Point State Park, but a Michigan Recreation Passport is not required for parking.

15 Whitefish Point Light Station

Great Lakes Shipwreck Museum, 18335 N. Whitefish Point Road, Paradise 49768;
(888) 492-3747
shipwreckmuseum.com/shipwreck-museum/whitefish-point-light

This lighthouse, in service since 1849, is connected with the Great Lakes Shipwreck Museum and also is next to the Whitefish Point Bird Observatory, making a visit here one of the most enjoyable and diverse days for lighthouse fans. Located on a beautiful spit of land, this lighthouse occupies a crucial point in navigation along what is known as Lake Superior's Shipwreck Coast. It is close to the site where the *Edmund Fitzgerald* went down. It is a fascinating part of history, and along with the keeper's house, it makes for a very accessible destination.

Mineral-stained cliffs of Pictured Rocks

MICHIGAN IS A LAND of contrasts, and rock hounds can enjoy this variety by wandering beaches and collecting agates and Petoskey stones, taking tours of iron and copper mines, and taking in the colorful scenery of Pictured Rocks National Lakeshore. At Pictured Rocks, there are patterns in the sandstones and limestones unlike those found anywhere else. With all this and more, Michigan has much to offer visitors interested in rock-hounding, mining, or geology.

ROCKS & MINERALS

2 Various locations

Rocks &
Minerals

1 A. E. Seaman Mineral Museum

Michigan Tech University, 1404 E. Sharon Ave., Houghton 49931; (906) 487-2572
museum.mtu.edu

Leave it to a Michigan university to pull together the most gorgeous collection of Michigan minerals. Whether they are metallic, fluorescent, or precious gems, these specimens are works of art. If the mining tours have sparked your interest in rocks and minerals, then this museum has what you need. Named after a geology professor, this museum houses 40,000-plus specimens, most of which represent the Great Lakes region. The star here is the 19-ton Lake Copper specimen, which holds the world record for the largest piece of native copper.

2 Agate Collecting

Lake Superior's shoreline and glacial gravel deposits
superiortrails.com/rock-hound.html, exploringthenorth.com/rocks/collect.html

Over a billion years ago, an immense amount of lava cooled in what would become the Lake Superior basin. As this lava cooled, volcanic gases were trapped in the lava, forming small cavities. Eventually, silica-infused water seeped into these cavities, leading to the formation of Lake Superior agates. These popular gemstones exhibit concentric or parallel banding and are often tinted in rich hues of red, yellow, and orange. Millions of years after the agates formed, glaciers bulldozed their way across the region, uncovering the long-buried agates and transporting them across a wide area. Since then, water and waves have further distributed these stones, and they can be found on rocky shores and at gravel pits. Agates are smooth and hard and polish to a brilliant sheen. In fact, that's one way to spot them. When you're hunting, look for rocks that are waxy-looking and often pitted.

3 Cliffs Shaft Mine Museum

501 W. Euclid St., Ishpeming 49849; (906) 485-1882
facebook.com/cliffsshaft

Iron mining in the U.P. dates back to the mid-1800s. The Cliffs Shaft mine began producing ore after the Civil War, but it wasn't until later that the mine gained its claim to fame: the massive obelisks that are now placed in front of the A and B shafts. These Egyptian Revival obelisks came into being when the old wooden headframes needed replacing in 1919. The company decided that the new structure should make an architectural statement, and so architect George Washington Maher designed two concrete Egyptian Revival obelisks to be placed at both the A and B shafts. These obelisks became a symbol of Ishpeming itself. Mining ceased in 1967, but today the site is preserved for the visiting public. Its many artifacts and unique stories help convey the unique history of the area.

4 Coppertown USA Mining Museum

25815 Red Jacket Road, Calumet 49913; (906) 337-4354; off-season inquiries: (800) 338-7982
uppermichigan.com/coppertown, keweenawheritagesites.org/site-coppertown.php

The history of copper mining in Michigan dates back to American Indians who collected exposed copper and dug trenches to expose underground copper veins. They beat the copper, shaped it, and used it for a number of purposes. Eventually, men like Douglass Houghton traveled to Lake Superior's wild shoreline in search of mineral wealth. In subsequent years, miners and engineers learned how to extract the ore from the ground more efficiently. In so doing, towns were built, lives were lost, and a rich history was written. With artifacts and well-constructed exhibits of these times, Coppertown Mining Museum tells the story of Michigan's long mining history. You'll find artifacts and stories in this museum, including an exhibit on labor leader Annie Clemenc and the Italian Hall Disaster. The museum is open from June through mid-October.

5 Delaware Copper Mine Tours

7804 Delaware Mine Road, Mohawk 49950; (906) 289-4688
delawarecopperminetours.com

One of the earliest mines in the Keweenaw Peninsula, the Delaware Copper Mine operated from 1847 to 1887 and produced 8 million pounds of copper. Today's visitors can take a self-guided tour of the mine's first level, 100 feet below the surface, to see where American copper mining began. Pure veins of copper are exposed in the walls, along with other geological interests. Aboveground, walking trails pass mine ruins, antique engines, mining equipment, and a petting zoo. A prehistoric mining pit is also located on the grounds. Pets are welcome on tours, too! Delaware Copper Mine is a Keweenaw Heritage Site and is open June through October.

6 Keweenaw National Historical Park

Calumet Visitor Center 98 Fifth St., Calumet 49913; (906) 337-3168
nps.gov/kewe

It is hard to explain Keweenaw National Historical Park. Unlike other parks, it does not own all of the resources that it encompasses. It's a collaborative park, one where the National Park Service partners with existing tour operators and even historic communities (such as Calumet) to tell a regional story of national importance. The park is primarily focused on the history of copper mining and the people, primarily Finnish and Cornish immigrants, who were the primary workforce of the mines. To get started, head to the Calumet Visitor Center near downtown Calumet; it has information about what to see, exhibits, historic photos, as well as a gift shop.

7 Menominee Range Historical Museum/Cornish Pumping Engine & Mining Museum

Historical Museum 300 E. Ludington St., Iron Mountain 49801; (906) 774-4276

Pumping Engine & Mining Museum 300 Kent St., Iron Mountain 49801;
(906) 774-1086
menomineemuseum.com

Named for the Menominee River, which separates the U.P. from northeastern Wisconsin, the mineral-rich Menominee Iron Range covers an area from eastern Dickinson County, Michigan, through Florence County, Wisconsin, and up through Iron County, Michigan. The Menominee Range Historical Museum, located in the former Carnegie Public Library, is listed as a Michigan Historic Site and is home to a wide variety of exhibits pertaining to local history. The Cornish Pumping Engine & Mining Museum is a must-see for the mechanically inclined, as it's home to the largest steam-driven pumping engine ever constructed in the U.S., and one of the largest in the world. Mining collectors… and history buffs alike will find these museums, both operated by the Menominee Range Historical Foundation, to be of special interest.

8 | Michigan Iron Industry Museum

73 Forge Road, Negaunee 49866; (906) 475-7857
michigan.gov/ironindustrymuseum

This museum is fascinating both because of its content and its location on the Carp River Forge, at the site of the first iron forge in the area. The site is beautiful, but it is also a reminder of what the landscape looked like before mining. Inside, the exhibits tell the story of mining and also the stories of the miners themselves. The miners worked hard under difficult conditions, but the wealth generated by the mines didn't flow back to them. These were people who sacrificed, but survived. Their stories are fascinating, and so is the history of mining and the advancement of mining technology. If you want to spend some time outside as well, this museum is at the trailhead of the 47-mile Iron Ore Heritage Trail.

9 | Old Victoria Copper Mine and Restoration Site

25401 Victoria Dam Road, Rockland 49960; (906) 886-2617
facebook.com/oldvictoria, exploringthenorth.com/oldvictoria/mine.html

At Old Victoria, you can get a closer look at the day-to-day lives of miners and their families from one mining company town. This site, however, focuses less on the mines and more on what it was like to live in a community of miners. Restorations are ongoing, but tours are currently offered through a number of structures, including a boarding house and a few single-family homes. With abandoned homes and relics still on the ground, sites like these have a different feel than designed exhibits. You can almost hear the echo of history as you look at these remnants of past lives.

0 | Petoskey Stone Collecting

Northwest Lower Peninsula's stony beaches and gravel areas
petoskeyarea.com/petoskey-stone-73, geo.msu.edu/extra/geogmich/petoskystone.html

The great museums in Michigan house a number of treasures, but sometimes you want to do some treasure hunting of your own. In the northwestern part of the Lower Peninsula, with all of its shops, trails, and restaurants, a small stone is the elusive prize. Petoskey stones are fossils of small corals (*Hexagonaria percarinata*) that lived during the Devonian period (350 million years ago). Much later, these fossils were scattered around the area by glaciers. As their scientific name suggests, hexagonal patterns mark the coral, giving it a distinctive quality that collectors love. Finding Petoskey stones on Michigan's rocky

beaches is fun and rewarding, and while it can be difficult to spot them, searching for them is a popular pastime. In fact, the Petoskey stone is so popular that it was named the state stone of Michigan in 1965. If you can't find them yourself, Petoskey stones are found in jewelry stores, gift shops, and museums. And if you *really* like this kind of adventure, you could always attend the annual Petoskey Stone Festival (see next profile).

Note: The Michigan Department of Natural Resources (DNR), which supervises Michigan's state parks, prohibits gathering more than 25 pounds of stones per visit, and the DNR reserves the right to confiscate individual stones weighing more than 25 pounds each. You'll also need a Michigan Recreation Passport to hunt for stones in Michigan state parks (see page 5 for more information). In addition, you can't take home Petoskey stones that you find on National Park Service lands such as Sleeping Bear Dunes National Lakeshore.

11 Petoskey Stone Festival

Barnes Park Campground 12298 Barnes Park Road, Eastport 49627, (231) 599-2712; festival information: (231) 533-8818
antrimcounty.org/barnespark.asp, petoskeystonefestival.com

Each year in Eastport on Memorial Day weekend, the Petoskey Stone Festival features Michigan's state stone. The festival includes a 5K race, a stone skipping contest, various demonstrations, local vendors, and a Petoskey stone hunt. Check the festival website for dates and a full list of activities.

12 Pictured Rocks National Lakeshore

Munising Falls Visitor Center (open year-round) 1505 Sand Point Road, Munising 49862; (906) 387-3700

Grand Sable Visitor Center (open summer only) E21090 County Road H-58, Seney; (906) 494-2660
nps.gov/piro

Pictured Rocks National Lakeshore is home to more than 15 miles of mineral-stained rock and cliff formations. These naturally sculptured wonders tell an important geological story. As you walk through the trails and explore the layered rocks, you can walk past rocks that differ widely in age. The oldest formations feature rocks from the

Precambrian period (which ended more than 540 million years ago). Then the geology makes a tremendous leap; instead of hundreds of millions of years old, the newer geological features are from the last 2 million years. Each rock unit here has a different hardness, and this means each one weathers differently, leading to the celebrated shapes of the Pictured Rocks. Chapel Rock and Miners Castle are just a sample of the dramatic rock formations in the park.

3 Quincy Mine Hoist Association Tours

49750 US 41, Hancock 49930; (906) 482-3101
quincymine.com

The Quincy Mine is one of the most imposing and impressive sites near the towns of Houghton and Hancock. Like an ancient sculpture garden, this mine is set amid picturesque ruins from mining's heyday, and some of the mining artifacts look like large metal sculptures. Walking the ruins is fascinating, but going on the underground tour right into the mine is the most intriguing part of a visit. Here, with the dark shafts, artificial lights, and a tour guide you will get a sense of what copper mining was like here from 1868 to 1920.

Petoskey Stones are the main draw at the Petoskey Stone Festival

The Selfridge Military Museum is located at Selfridge Air National Guard Base, home to A-10 Warthogs

WHEN IT COMES TO MICHIGAN, cars, trucks, and ships are undoubtedly the stars of the show, but they aren't the only ways to get around the Mitten State. Michigan also has an impressive history of air and rail travel, and these sites are great places to explore and make for wonderful day trips. In these places your travel will be both figurative and literal as you explore Michigan's rich transportation history.

RAILROADS & AIRPLANES

2 Various locations

1 Air Zoo Aerospace & Science Experience

Flight Innovation Center 6151 Portage Road, Portage 49002; (269) 382-6555, (866) 524-7966

Flight Discovery Center 3101 E. Milham Road, Kalamazoo, 49002
airzoo.org

Though the name may lead you to believe otherwise, this imaginative museum and amusement facility isn't just about aircraft. While it is home to a wonderful collection of airplanes and a great place to learn about the history of aviation (in both war and peacetime), this museum also features craft that have ventured into space. Go to the Michigan Aviation Hall of Fame and gain an appreciation for the people who have connected us to outer space. You can walk around, observe, and take in the history that is here—but even better, get on the rides and have fun. If you've ever wanted to fly, try out the flight simulators.

2 Amtrak

Blue Water Runs between Chicago and Port Huron

Pere Marquette Runs between Chicago and Grand Rapids

Wolverine Runs between Chicago and Pontiac

amtrak.com/michigan-services-train, amtrak.com/trails-rails-heritage-appreciation-during-your-train-ride

Several Amtrak routes connect Michigan cities to Chicago and provide a relaxing way to see the scenic landscape. All the lines make additional stops in the state as well, and a number of the trips in this book are located near the train lines. Check Amtrak's website for the most up-to-date schedule information.

3 Crossroads Village and Huckleberry Railroad

6140 Bray Road, Flint 48505; (810) 736-7100
geneseecountyparks.org/crossroads-village

The Huckleberry Railroad first began to operate in the late 1850s. Now it is a heritage railroad rather than a functional line, and

40-minute rides are available out of Crossroads Village. The Huckleberry Railroad was known for being quite slow—it got its name because passengers supposedly had time during a trip to get off the moving railroad car, pick a few huckleberries, and get back on again. After your ride on the railroad, continue your trip into the past by exploring Crossroads Village with its historical buildings and interpretive craftspeople.

4 Little River Railroad: Coldwater to Quincy

29 W. Park Ave., Coldwater 49036; (517) 227-5488
littleriverrailroad.com

Even in this age of computers and jets, there is something romantic about railroads—not just the modern high-speed trains, but the old steam engines chugging along and puffing white smoke into the blue sky. Lucky for us, steam engines aren't only found in history books; you can still catch a ride on one at the Little River Railroad, which runs between Coldwater and Quincy. The ride lasts approximately 1 hour and 45 minutes, so climb on board and settle in. Check out the railroad's website for special-event options that coincide with community events along the way.

5 Michigan Transit Museum

200 Grand Ave., Mount Clemens 48043; (586) 463-1863
michigantransitmuseum.org

No railroad system could operate without depots, and that's especially true for passenger lines. This museum is located in the restored depot where Thomas Edison began a brief railroading career. Looking as pristine as it did in 1900, it holds displays from that same era, giving visitors a sense of both history and what railroading was like. The depot was in use until 1980 and while you can no longer catch a train from here, you can take a short ride on Sundays from nearby Henry B. Joy Boulevard. Note that the depot is open only on weekends, and the train rides run only on Sundays. (*Note:* Closed at the time of this writing; check website for updates.)

Selfridge Military Air Museum

Selfridge Air National Guard Base 27333 C St., Harrison Township 48045; (586) 239-5035
selfridgeairmuseum.org

This is an active military base that offers visitor access. Here you can see a collection of restored military aircraft on display and a collection of exhibits that show the importance of airplanes throughout the military history of the United States. This is an outreach effort

of the Michigan Air Guard Historical Association, and it honors this important branch of the Armed Forces. It also honors all those men and women who served America and lost their lives due to their gallant efforts. It is both an inspiring and sobering history. *Note:* Because the museum is inside a military base, U.S. citizens must pass a security background check or present a U.S. government ID card before they can enter; see the website for more details.

7 Tahquamenon Falls Train and Riverboat Tours

7195 County Road 381, Soo Junction, 49868; (888) 778-7246; depot: (906) 876-2311 trainandboattours.com

Now here's an idea: how about a 6½-hour trip through the wild forests of the U.P., including a train ride, a riverboat cruise, and a brief hike to one of the nation's most beautiful waterfalls? The falls are located on the beautiful and wild Tahquamenon River. If you'd prefer to avoid the boat trip, you can choose to just do the railroad ride, but for a full-day trip, this is hard to beat. People have been taking this unusual tour since 1927, and the scenery and the stories continue to entertain and impress. Bear, moose, otters, and migratory birds may make their appearances anywhere along the route.

8 Yankee Air Museum

47884 D St., Belleville 48111; (734) 483-4030 yankeeairmuseum.org

Did you know that Ford once manufactured airplanes? If not, here is a fun way for you to learn more about aviation. In 1941, this airfield was constructed to serve the B-24 bombers that were manufactured using Ford's mass-production techniques. At its height, the factory produced 1 bomber every 59 minutes. This museum and collection was devastated by fire in 2004, but the airplanes in flying condition were saved. Come in, look around, and enjoy an air show, but if you want the most from your visit, book a flight on one of the historic aircraft. Work on the new Roush Aeronautics Center is also currently underway.

A B-24 Liberator, once produced at what is now the Yankee Air Museum

Ann Arbor Hands-on Museum

MICHIGAN HAS A wonderful array of nature centers and museums that are devoted to helping visitors understand science and better connect with the world around them. The great thing about these trips is that they aren't passive. You get to participate, both mentally and physically, and the result is a satisfying and fun experience.

SCIENCE MUSEUMS & NATURE CENTERS

(continued on next page)

154

ady Slipper Orchids are celebrated at Huron County Nature Center

1 Ann Arbor Hands-On Museum

220 E. Ann St., Ann Arbor 48104; (734) 995-5439
aahom.org

If the key to learning is being engaged, then this museum will connect you and your family with science. This museum and a science center combined is a place to bring the whole family to share experiences, ask questions, experiment, and learn. The exhibits change over time, and many explore the concepts that are needed for more complex scientific inquiry, such topics as weather, light, optics, and bubbles. Check the website for information on special exhibits and events.

2 Blandford Nature Center

1715 Hillburn Ave. NW, Grand Rapids 49504; (616) 735-6240
blandfordnaturecenter.org

An urban oasis that brings kids, families, and adults together, this nature center is home to a farm, trails, and a host of educational programs led by naturalists. The center consists of 143 acres in the middle of an urban area and features a visitor center, a wildlife education center, a farm, and hiking trails, giving the visitor many options for a day of exploring. Like so many nature centers, this has become a refuge for injured wildlife that cannot be released into the wild. These animal ambassadors supplement the natural diversity of the landscape and are an excellent way to help kids make connections with nature. To get the full flavor of the center, don't go just once—plan a visit for each of the four seasons.

3 Chippewa Nature Center

400 S. Badour Road, Midland 48640; (989) 631-0830
chippewanaturecenter.org

Located across the river from downtown Midland, this nature center includes part of the Chippewa Trail, so you can explore by both foot and bike on the center's 19 miles of trails. They also offer Nature Preschool and a Nature Day Camp, along with numerous special programs for adults and families. Features of the center include the Bur Oak Theater, where visitors can watch a series of short informational films; the River Overlook, which has a stunning view of the Pine and Chippewa Rivers; the Wildlife Viewing Area, where spectators can watch the antics of animals at the feeders through one-way glass; and the hands-on, kid-friendly Nature Discovery area, which includes books, animal pelts, microscopes, and more. The visitor center is open seven days a week with free admission save for during a few popular events.

Cranbrook Institute of Science

39221 Woodward Ave., Bloomfield Hills 48303; (248) 645-3200, (877) 462-7262
science.cranbrook.edu

This institute provides a great place to learn about science, technology, and natural history. There are well-designed exhibits, hands-on activities, and planetarium shows, plus you can have a picnic or eat at the café to make this a day-long visit. Here you can learn about the distant stars in the sky or, for something a little closer to home, visit the Erb Family Science Garden. The institute's programs vary by season, allowing the process of discovery to go on and on.

Curious Kids' Museum and Discovery Zone

Museum 415 Lake Blvd., St. Joseph 49085; (269) 983-2543

Discovery Zone 333 Broad St., St. Joseph 49085; (269) 982-8500
curiouskidsmuseum.org

Science is serious, right? Well, yes and no. Science begins with fun, an invitation to explore and investigate, and the encouragement to experiment. Located on a bluff overlooking Lake Michigan, the Curious Kids' Museum is the place for kids to begin to learn about science. Each floor is filled with learning opportunities, games, and exhibits—but don't think the fun ends when you leave the building. You can enjoy Silver Beach and the great Whirlpool Compass Fountain across the street or stroll along the bluff's History Trail. If you want to go all-out, though, you should definitely make sure to also see the nearby Discovery Zone at Silver Beach Center, which is perfect for all kids, from toddlers to teens.

Fenner Nature Center

2020 E. Mount Hope Ave., Lansing 48910; (517) 483-4224
mynaturecenter.org

There are more than 4 miles of trails in this 134-acre preserve, including two paved loops for mobility-impaired visitors. The nature center also has live animals and interpretive displays, and it also hosts a number of annual festivals and many special programs for all ages. Admission is free, but a small donation is suggested.

7 Hemlock Crossing Park and Nature Education Center

8115 W. Olive Road, West Olive 49460; (616) 738-4810
miottawa.org/Parks/hemlockcrossing.htm

With nearly 240 acres along the Pigeon River in Ottawa County, there is ample room here to hike, snowshoe, cross-country ski, and watch for animals. Also be sure to stop by the Nature Education Center at the park to learn about the local environment and history and to see animals at the Wildlife Viewing Area. The site offers snowshoe rental, a nature center, a kayak and canoe launch, and picnic areas. Don't miss the pedestrian bridge, which offers wonderful views of the river.

8 Huron County Nature Center

3336 Loosemore Road, Port Austin 48467; (989) 551-8400
huronnaturecenter.org

It's rare to find a piece of untouched land—but that's what you get at the Huron County Nature Center. First preserved as 120 acres in 1941 by the Women's Club of Huron County, today the center comprises 280 acres of diverse habitats. From dry and sandy swales to old hardwood forests, there's just so much to see here. Visit the Center's website before arriving to learn more about the various habitats and what you're able to see and do in each.

9 Impression 5 Science Center

200 Museum Drive, Lansing 48933; (517) 485-8116
impression5.org

There's plenty to see at Impression 5 Science Center, but if you only look at the exhibits, you're missing out on the full experience. This hands-on museum is meant to be explored with all five senses. Learn about water and fluid dynamics in the two-story FLOW exhibit, or create your own light mosaic in the electromagnetic spectrum. The exhibits aim to create opportunities for playing problem-solving, and risk-taking for the whole family.

John and Mary Dahlem Environmental Education Center

7117 S. Jackson Road, Jackson 49201; (517) 782-3453
dahlemcenter.org

Located on nearly 300 acres, the Dahlem Environmental Center offers visitors 5 miles of walking trails to enjoy. The trails wander through a variety of habitats, from open grassland and oak savannas to fens, ponds, woods, and farmland. The Nature for All Trail provides an approximately quarter-mile nature experience for visitors with limited mobility (wheelchairs, walkers, strollers), and a Nature Playscape offers free play opportunities for children of all ages in a safe environment. The property includes the Dahlem Ecology Farm, which features a community garden, a public apiary and a butterfly trail. Dahlem is a wonderful place for birding and botanizing, and nature classes are offered year-round for children or all ages.

Kalamazoo Nature Center

7000 N. Westnedge Ave., Kalamazoo 49009; (269) 381-1574
naturecenter.org

Whether you want to learn about rural and farm living or experience nature and all its variation, this center is a treasure. The main campus of the nature center, on more than 1,100 acres of land, has plenty to see and do. Stop by the award-winning visitor center, explore the more than 14 miles of trails, or stop to visit DeLano Farms. If you want something a little more structured, sign up for one of the various educational programs that run in all seasons and for all ages. If your interests run toward art as much as nature, you should also try the self-guided sculpture tour and see how many of the figures you can discover.

Kalamazoo Valley Museum

230 N. Rose St., Kalamazoo 49007; (800) 772-3370, (269) 373-7990
kalamazoomuseum.org

This museum is the perfect place to get kids interested in science and history. Preschool-age children can let their imaginations run wild in the Children's Landscape, a space designed specially for them. Older kids will love the Science on a Sphere exhibit, where images of environmental processes are projected onto a massive globe screen and which was designed by weather and climate specialists. Other permanent exhibits include favorites such as the Kalamazoo Direct to You history gallery and Mystery of the Mummy, featuring a 2,300-year-old Egyptian mummy! Special traveling exhibits change often, so there's always something new to see and do. With tons of activities and hands-on interactivities, the Kalamazoo Valley Museum makes learning fun!

Science Museums & Nature Centers

13 Sarett Nature Center

2300 Benton Center Road, Benton Harbor 49022; (269) 927-4832
sarett.com

Located along the Paw Paw River, this 1,000-acre education center is a place for the whole family. Eight miles of trails, interpretive programs, and even a treetop walkway provide many reasons to visit. If you're wondering what to do on your visit, head to the visitor center; there's also a butterfly house (in season) and a nature play area. If you enjoy geocaching, the center has multiple permanent caches and provides rental GPS units to help you find them.

14 Seven Ponds Nature Center

3854 Crawford Road, Dryden 48428; (810) 796-3200
sevenponds.org

This nature center's many ponds attract birds and wildlife and provide an excellent classroom in which to learn about the natural world and the importance of fresh water. From winter bird counts to guided hikes, there are many ways for visitors of all ages to explore. If the weather doesn't cooperate on your visit, there's still plenty to see and do in the interpretive center, including an observation beehive, a beaver lodge, and a library of nature books and periodicals.

15 Sloan Museum and Longway Planetarium

Sloan Museum   4190 E. Court St., Burton 48509; (810) 237-3450

Longway Planetarium   1310 E. Kearsley St., Flint 48503; (810) 237-3400
sloanlongway.org

If you want a high-quality learning experience that is also eclectic, this is your destination. There are two facilities here: the Sloan Museum at Courtland and the Longway Planetarium. The museum, which has been undergoing an expansion and renovation, covers a wide variety of subjects and features traveling science and children's exhibits. You can also see over 80 years of Buick cars and trucks made all, or in part, in the Flint area. All of this variety makes it possible to enjoy a full day here. Check the website to see current programs and showtimes for the planetarium.

16 Upper Peninsula Children's Museum

123 W. Baraga Ave., Marquette 49855; (906) 226-3911
upchildrensmuseum.org

When a setting is imaginative and engaging, play turns to learning. At this arts and sciences museum, there are many hands-on activities that cover everything from aviation and car mechanics to health and nutrition. If you want a little something extra when you visit, aim for the monthly Creative Series, featuring music, food, and crafts. With such a variety, kids (and adults) can't help but have fun at this museum.

17 Woldumar Nature Center

5739 Old Lansing Road, Lansing 48917; (517) 322-0030
woldumar.org

With more than 5 miles of trails and a variety of diverse ecosystems, Woldumar Nature Center offers numerous options for hiking, cross-country skiing, and bird-watching. The grounds include an herb garden, a blacksmith shop, and one of the oldest residences in Eaton County, the 1860 Moon Log Cabin. There are several special events at the center, including the American Heritage Festival, a fall Colors Tour on the river, and an annual 5K and 10K Trail Run.

A heavily wooded trail at Woldumar Nature Center

Coaster II

WHEN JOHN MASEFIELD wrote the famous lines, "I must go down to the seas again, to the lonely sea and the sky, / And all I ask is a tall ship and a star to steer her by," he might not have had Michigan in mind, but had he visited some of the exciting ship-related stops Michigan has to offer, he might have changed the line to, "I must go down to the Lakes again." And, of course, if you're familiar with Michigan, you already know all about the deep blue waters of the Great Lakes, which are home to hundreds of shipwrecks and nautical attractions.

SHIPS & SHIPWRECKS

(continued on next page)

The Great Lakes Shipwreck Museum

1 Alpena Shipwreck Tours

500 W. Fletcher St., Alpena 49707; (888) 469-4696, (989) 884-6200
thunderbayfriends.org/index.php/alpena-shipwreck-tours

This is Lake Huron's Shipwreck Alley, and you can explore the shipwrecks yourself even if you don't scuba dive. Thunder Bay National Marine Sanctuary sells tickets on the 65-foot-long *Lady Michigan,* a tour boat with large glass-bottom viewing wells. You can spend an afternoon on the water learning about the ships, the shore, and the lighthouses. Both outdoor and heated indoor seating are available for these seasonal cruises.

2 Aquastar Lake Cruises

560 Mart St., Muskegon 49440; (231) 903-0669, (800) 853-6311
aquastarcruises.com

This private charter business that offers public and private tours, it offers sightseeing trips and trips that include meals on board the *Aquastar* (formerly known as the *Port City Princess*). Climb aboard for an afternoon or sunset cruise, or, if you want to combine boating with a taste of local beverages, try the Pigeon Home Town Cruise or the Odd Side Ales Cruise. If you can make it out in August, stop by for the annual Blessing of the Boats event, which marks the beginning of another boating season. The boat can also accommodate private charters and events.

3 BaySail/Appledore Schooners

107 Fifth St., Bay City 48708; (989) 895-5193
baysailbaycity.org

The Appledore tall ships, the *Appledore IV* and *Appledore V,* sail out of downtown Bay City and into Saginaw Bay, where you can experience the thrill of setting sail and catching the wind. You don't have to worry, though, as these sailboats are supported by modern navigation and safety equipment, so you can just participate and enjoy. There are private charters that can be arranged, or you can join one of the public sails. If you are looking for something special, try a port visit to a local event. If you plan ahead, you can be on board for the area's annual fireworks show.

4 Dossin Great Lakes Museum

100 Strand Drive, Belle Isle, Detroit 48207; (313) 833-1805
detroithistorical.org/dossin-great-lakes-museum/plan-your-visit/general
-information

When you enter through the Gothic Room, a reconstructed lounge from
the *City of Detroit III,* be prepared for opulence. This is probably not
what you would expect from a shipping museum, but in the early 1900s,
when a room much like this was in use, industrial giants rode in style on
this ship between Detroit and Cleveland or Buffalo. The museum, operated by the Detroit Historical Society, also features the SS *William Clay
Ford* pilot house; here, kids and adults can get a sense of what it might
feel like to be in charge of one of the large vessels of the Great Lakes.
And don't miss the newly overhauled main exhibit, Built by the River,
which discusses the relationship among Detroit, the Detroit River, and
the Great Lakes. *Note:* You will need a Michigan Recreation Passport
(see page 5) to visit this museum, which is part of Belle Isle Park.

5 Great Lakes Lore Maritime Museum

367 N. Third St., Rogers City 49779; (989) 734-0706
gllmm.com

This is a hall of fame for the working people who have served the
shipping industry. The museum honors its inductees with a ceremony
and a collage that features their pictures, their history, and the ships
on which they sailed. The museum also features a collection of artifacts, displays about American Indians, fur traders, lighthouse keepers,
and model ships, but the museum's true focus is on preserving the
memories behind the artifacts. If you visit, consider a trip in August,
when the museum celebrates its inductees, allowing a very personal
look at the Great Lakes sailors.

Great Lakes Maritime Center

51 Court St., Port Huron 48060; (810) 985-4817
achesonventures.com/maritime-center

The Great Lakes Maritime Center is a great vantage point for ship
watching, but it's also a place to learn about the history of shipping
on the Great Lakes. Inside, videos and exhibits tell the stories, but if
you want to learn more, you can also time your visit to coincide with
one of their speaker programs. At the center, you can also check out
the world headquarters of BoatNerd.com (the premier website on
Great Lakes shipping), where you can get all your boat-related questions answered. After you've spent some time indoors, go outside to
the walkway and ship-watch with your binoculars.

7 Great Lakes Shipwreck Museum

18335 N. Whitefish Point Road, Paradise 49768; (888) 492-3747
shipwreckmuseum.com

Located at the Whitefish Point Light Station and next door to the Whitefish Point Bird Observatory, this destination will definitely require a day to explore. Gordon Lightfoot's "The Wreck of the *Edmund Fitzgerald*" is probably the most well-known song about the Great Lakes, and if that song still lingers in your mind, this is the place to learn what happened. The story of the *Edmund Fitzgerald*—sunk during a terrible Lake Superior gale on November 9, 1975—is told in detail here, along with the stories of many other wrecks. Artifacts, recovered relics, videos, a collection of models, and displays help tell these haunting but important stories.

One of the Edmund Fitzgerald's lifeboats on display at the Museum Ship Valley Camp

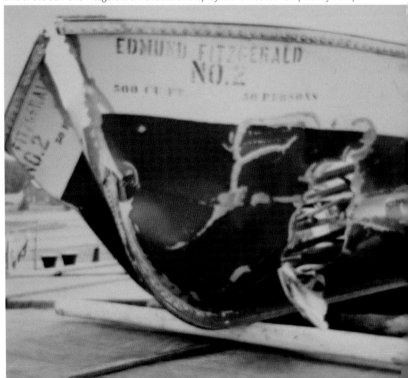

8 | Michigan Maritime Museum

260 Dyckman Ave., South Haven 49090; (269) 637-8078
michiganmaritimemuseum.org

Appropriately located on the shore of Lake Michigan, five separate
buildings offer opportunities for the museum visitor. The exhibits here
vary, but many are hands-on and all are inspiring and informative.
There's a research library as well as a center where visitors can sign up
for boat-building classes or classes pertaining to other maritime skills.
Whatever you do, visit often, as there are many special events and
speakers. Also, if you go down to the water, be sure to check out the
sloop *Friends Good Will* and the river launch *Lindy Lou.*

9 | Michigan Underwater Preserves

Various locations around Michigan
Michigan Department of Environment, Great Lakes, and Energy, 800-662-9278
tinyurl.com/michiganunderwaterpreserves

Each of the Great Lakes has a long history of shipwrecks, and Michigan
alone has countless shipwrecks. Certain parts of the lake are more
dangerous, and wrecks are often concentrated there, making such
sites worthy of a special trip. In Michigan, 13 underwater preserves
have been established to protect these historic sites, and today these
preserves cover more than 7,200 square miles of the Great Lakes. Of
course, diving in these areas can be dangerous, so you need to be very
well prepared before visiting them. In addition, if you visit, remember
that these are historic sites, so it goes without saying that you shouldn't
take anything from these sites. Show the wrecks (and future divers)
the respect they deserve.

0 | Museum Ship *Valley Camp*

501 E. Water St., Sault Ste. Marie 49783; (906) 632-3658, (888) 744-7867
saulthistoricsites.com/museum-ship-valley-camp

The *Valley Camp* was a lake freighter before she became a museum. The
ship offers tours of her deck and her cargo holds. If you can take your
eyes off the ship itself, the interior of the ship is a museum with more
than 20,000 square feet of space and more than 100 exhibits, including access to the crew quarters and the captain's quarters and four
large aquariums of native Great Lakes fish. The museum includes two
lifeboats from the *Edmund Fitzgerald* that tore away during the sinking
and were never used by the crew. You can also watch a video about the
infamous 1975 storm in which the great boat sank.

11 Pictured Rocks Cruises

100 City Park Drive, Munising 49862; (906) 387-2379
picturedrocks.com

One of the best ways to see Pictured Rocks National Lakeshore is by boat. These boats are small enough to enable visitors to get a good look at Pictured Rocks, but you're sheltered if Lake Superior acts up. On the ride out of the harbor, the staff will share stories of shipwrecks and lighthouses. Once you're out of the bay, visitors will ooh and aah at the wave-washed sandstone cliffs that are replete with colorful patterns and sculpted caves and bays. On these tours, there is plenty of time to take photos, and the captain navigates the waters with precision, enabling a close look. Try taking the ride at different times of day to see how light can change the view. When you're done, enter the park itself and see the cliffs from above.

12 Soo Locks Boat Tours

Dock #1 1157 E. Portage Ave., Sault Ste. Marie 49783; (906) 632-6301

Dock #2 515 E. Portage Ave., Sault Ste. Marie 49783; (906) 632-2512
soolocks.com, saultstemarie.com/attractions/soo-locks

A boat tour through the Soo Locks is the perfect way to marvel at the engineering feat that is the locks. These tours take place on the St. Marys River, which connects Lake Superior with Lake Huron and the remaining Great Lakes. All vessels going to or from Lake Superior have to pass through this bottleneck, and that makes these locks internationally significant. There are a few tour options available for visitors, but no matter which one you pick, you will get to experience the 21-foot elevation change between the two lakes and will get to learn about the history of the locks and the surrounding area. Check the website before you visit to see if there will be any special-event cruises offered when you plan to go.

13 Soo Locks Visitor Center and Observation Area

329 W. Portage Ave., Sault Ste. Marie 49783; Vessel Hotline: (906) 253-9290
lre.usace.army.mil/Missions/Recreation/soolocksvisitorcenter.aspx
saultstemarie.com/attractions/soo-locks

If cruising through the locks isn't your thing, there's still plenty for you to do at the Locks. Stop in at the Visitor Center and Observation Centerto learn about how their history and how they work. For instance, 90% of all iron-ore in the United States traverses these locks. And with nearly 10,000 "lockages" each year, you're likely to get to see one of the freighters pass through the locks as well. Check the information at the visitor center when you arrive to see which boats they expect that day. Be sure to check the calendar before you visit, however, as the locks are closed annually for repairs and maintenance from January 15 to March 25 (the Visitor Center is open from Mother's Day to mid-October).

14 *Star of Saugatuck* Boat Cruises

716 Water St. (PO Box 190), Saugatuck 49453; (269) 857-4261
saugatuckboatcruises.com

Forget the tall ships and freighters carrying iron-ore and go back in time on board a ship that Mark Twain would have been familiar with: a sternwheeler paddleboat. As the paddlewheels turn, they create a nice rhythm, enabling visitors to relax and see Saugatuck from a new angle. During the day, you can watch the bustling activity around you, and in the evening you can go for a sunset cruise on Lake Michigan. The upriver tour follows the Kalamazoo River to Lake Kalamazoo and then comes back downstream. Continuing downriver, you can see where the wreck of the *Singapore* lies beneath a sandy shoal. If the weather on Lake Michigan is good, you can even admire some of the region's fascinating lighthouses (including Holland's "Big Red") from the deck.

15 Superior Odyssey Sailing Adventures

102 E. Main St., Marquette 49855; (906) 361-3668
exploringthenorth.com/odyssey/sail.html

Come on board the *Coaster II,* a historic wooden-hulled gaff schooner with topsails, and let the wind take you along the rugged Lake Superior coast. Setting out from the Marquette Lower Harbor, this ship can take you on a variety of sailing trips—just pick which one is best for you. There are 2-hour-long trips (daylight or sunset) and a 4-hour-long trip to Presque Isle. Themed events and parties are available, too. No matter which trip you choose, the Captain will entertain you while providing you with a sailing experience you won't forget.

16 Thunder Bay National Marine Sanctuary at the Great Lakes Maritime Heritage Center

500 W. Fletcher St., Alpena 49707; (989) 884-6200
thunderbay.noaa.gov

The Thunder Bay National Marine Sanctuary—one of only 14 national marine sanctuaries, and the only one located in freshwater—preserves more than 100 historic shipwrecks in and around Thunder Bay. Located on Lake Huron, many of these shipwrecks are intact; they range in depth from a few inches to more than 200 feet below the surface. If you are interested in the history of shipwrecks, this is the place for you. The displays here are filled with hands-on exhibits and stunning visuals. You can even climb aboard a life-size replica of a wooden schooner! Many recreational opportunities exist in these sanctuary waters, including kayaking, snorkeling, and scuba diving. If you have the time and interest, consider visiting the Thunder Bay Sanctuary Research Collection, one of the largest archival collections of Great Lakes maritime history, located at the Alpena County George N. Fletcher Public Library.

17 Traverse Tall Ship Company

13258 S. West Bay Shore Drive, Traverse City 49684; (231) 941-2000, (800) 678-0383
tallshipsailing.com

Traverse City is home to wineries, bike trails, and quaint shops. It's also home to the schooner *Manitou,* which offers three different daily cruises. Sail in the morning with breakfast pastries and cocktails, or sample Moomers, a local ice cream, on the afternoon sails. In the evening, you can enjoy a sunset dinner cruise. If you want something more specific and personalized for your trip, look into charting the sailing yacht *Scout* for the day.

USS *Silversides* Submarine Museum

1346 Bluff St., Muskegon 49441; (231) 755-1230
silversidesmuseum.org

A real submarine from World War II and a Coast Guard cutter from the Prohibition era are anchored at the dock and waiting for you to get on board. Here is a chance to step onto (and into) a submarine for the crew members who would spend weeks living and working aboard the vessel. The USS *Silversides* was commissioned eight days after Pearl Harbor and was nicknamed "The Lucky Boat," as she sunk an astonishing 23 ships during her 14 war patrols. The sub was eventually declared a National Historic Landmark. The other boat here is a Coast Guard cutter, and it saw another form of action: during Prohibition, it patrolled the Great Lakes, a major route for the transportation of illegal liquor. If touring the exhibits, displays, and boat tours doesn't poop you out, turn your day trip into an overnighter and book a sleeping berth in the submarine itself.

The USS *Silversides* is now a floating museum

Tahquamenon Falls

THE PHYSICS OF WATERFALLS is simple to explain: water flows down a stream, the bedrock determines whether the river is flat or has falls, and gravity moves the water downhill and downstream. But that description doesn't explain the magic of falling water. If you like waterfalls, come to Michigan—its Upper Peninsula alone is home to more than 200 named waterfalls. Note, however, that optimal waterfall-viewing depends heavily on the weather, so check conditions before you go.

WATERFALLS

1 Agate Falls

Agate Falls Scenic Site, Trout Creek 49947; (906) 353-6558
tinyurl.com/agatefalls

An easy waterfall to see on the middle branch of the Ontonagon
River, Agate Falls is located at a scenic rest area. The view from
the bottom of the falls is really outstanding, though you'll have to
leave the main trail to get there. The river itself is 80 feet wide and
forested. A hiking bridge, which once carried a Duluth, South Shore,
and Atlantic Railway right-of-way, spans the falls. If you want to have
a picnic lunch, the rest area has tables. One note of warning: the trail
to the falls is steep and can be slippery. *Note:* Michigan Recreation
Passport required (see page 5).

Agate Falls

2 Alger Falls

East side of M-28, just outside the Munising city limits
gowaterfalling.com/waterfalls/alger.shtml

This is an easy falls to get to, located 1 mile south of Munising and just a few yards from M-28. Despite this, however, you can often find a bit of solitude here. Note that the water level of this falls can vary dramatically: if the weather has been dry lately, you might want to wait and visit again a different day.

3 Black River Falls

8 miles southwest of Ishpeming in Escanaba River State Forest; (906) 228-7749
gowaterfalling.com/waterfalls/blackriverfalls.shtml, michigan.org/property/black
-river-falls, travelmarquette.com/outdoor-adventure/waterfalls

Dropping nearly 30 feet through a narrow rock channel, this falls churns and foams more than most Michigan waterfalls. The falls are a quick hike along a short scenic path that's bordered by impressive pine trees. The hike is generally easy, though closer to the river the path gets steeper and there are river stones to navigate. The waterfalls can be viewed from a small island at the center of the river, which is easy to reach thanks to a footbridge.

4 Bond Falls

Bond Falls Scenic Site, Bond Falls Road, Paulding 49912; (906) 353-6558
tinyurl.com/bondfalls

As there are so many beautiful waterfalls in Michigan, it is hard to dub any one of them as the "best" in the state, but many put Bond Falls at the top of the list. Bond Falls is on the middle branch of the Ontonagon River and tumbles over a thick belt of fractured rock, with a drop of 40 feet. The falls have an accessible walkway with six viewing locations. The site also has roadside parking, and there are tables where you can enjoy a midday picnic. *Note:* Michigan Recreation Passport required (see page 5).

Canyon Falls

10 miles south of L'Anse on US 41; Alberta 49946; (800) 743-4908, (906) 524-7444
michigan.org/property/canyon-falls

After you park your car at the roadside park, it's about a 10-minute walk to the falls. The trail will take you over Bacco Creek and along the Sturgeon River passing by a few smaller waterfalls, but you shouldn't stop once you get to the Canyon Falls. Instead, continue downstream to the box-canyon gorge area, which has inspired the nickname "the Grand Canyon of the U.P."

Waterfalls

6 Manabezho Falls

Follow County Highway 519 to the west entrance of Porcupine Mountains State Park, then follow the signs; (906) 885-5725
gowaterfalling.com/waterfalls/manabezho.shtml, porcupineup.com/presque-isle -river-waterfalls, tinyurl.com/porcupinemtnsstatepark

On the west side of Porcupine Mountains Wilderness State Park, the Presque Isle River comes to a spectacular end that features shoots, rapids, falls, and an island that can be reached by a small pedestrian bridge. Manabezho Falls is the largest waterfall on this wonderful river. The falls themselves are not far from a parking lot, but you will need to climb some steps to reach them. If you want a longer hike, continue on past Manido and Nawadaha Falls to make the full 2.3-mile loop. *Note:* Michigan Recreation Passport required (see page 5).

7 Munising Falls, Pictured Rocks National Lakeshore

Munising Falls Visitor Center 1505 Sand Point Road, Munising 49862; (906) 387-3700
nps.gov/piro/planyourvisit/waterfalls.htm, gowaterfalling.com/waterfalls /munising.shtml

Munising Creek has a spectacular ending. It falls 50 feet over a lip of sandstone and past a crescent-shaped rock cliff that has been eroded by years of water flow. Even better, thanks to a paved walkway of only 800 feet, this waterfall is incredibly easy to visit. Nearby are an interpretive center, ample parking, and occasional park-ranger programs. And because the falls are so easy to access, they make for a good wintertime trip where you can see the falls frozen into an elongated column of ice.

Waterfalls

Sable Falls, Pictured Rocks National Lakeshore

About 1 mile west of Grand Marais on County Road H-58

Grand Sable Visitor Center E21090 County Road H-58; (906) 494-2660
nps.gov/piro/planyourvisit/waterfalls.htm

On the eastern border of Pictured Rocks National Lakeshore, this waterfall is located in a deep valley. Even though the falls are relatively small, they are still dramatic, as the water moves past big boulders and follows a natural stairway to the lake. Approach the falls from the national park trail, and take the stairs that start inland—but be aware that the drive to get here can be rough. If you want an easier drive but a longer walk, start at the Grand Sable Visitor Center and follow the Beech Forest Trail up to the falls.

Sable Falls

Waterfalls

9 Spray Falls and Bridalveil Falls, Pictured Rocks National Lakeshore

Interagency Visitor Center (year-round) 400 E. Munising Ave., Munising 49862; (906) 387-3700
nps.gov/piro/planyourvisit/waterfalls.htm

Pictured Rocks Cruises 100 City Park Drive, Munising 49862; (906) 387-2379
picturedrocks.com

These magnificent waterfalls originate as small streams that run through Pictured Rocks National Lakeshore and exit from the top of the cliffs straight into Lake Superior. Spray Falls is a free-fall waterfall, while Bridalveil Falls flows down a sloping cliff face. Bridalveil is a seasonal waterfall that is often little more than a trickle in late-summer and fall. These are some of the most dramatic waterfalls in Michigan because of the spectacular surroundings, and they are best viewed from the water. Pictured Rocks Cruises' boat tours take you out for a wonderful lakeside view that captures the grandeur of the panorama and sea kayaks get you in close and even wet (but be careful because rocks can accompany the water). There are limited opportunities to view Spray Falls from the North Country Trail, but you won't be able to see Bridalveil Falls at all while hiking. Check the weather, because the view is best after a good rain.

10 Tahquamenon Falls State Park

41382 W. M-123, Paradise 49768; (906) 492-3415
tinyurl.com/tahquamenonfalls

This park encompasses almost 50,000 acres of wild beauty and provides access to the magnificent Upper and Lower Falls. In terms of volume, Tahquamenon is the third-largest falls east of the Mississippi River. Lower Falls consists of a series of five drops that cascade around an island. The Upper Falls, four miles upstream from the Lower Falls, is 200 feet wide and 48 feet high with up to an estimated water flow of 50,000 gallons of water per second. Steps lead down to the falls, and there is a fully accessible trail and many place to get pictures of the canyon and falls. *Note:* Michigan Recreation Passport required (see page 5).

Waterfalls

11 Waterfalls of the Black River National Forest Scenic Byway

Ottawa National Forest Supervisor's Office, E6248 US 2, Ironwood 49938; (906) 932-1330

explorewesternup.com/things-to-do/black-river-area

Black River Falls isn't the only scenic waterfall on the Black River. To see a collection of falls, head to the Black River National Forest Scenic Byway, which has trails you can use to explore a number of them. (The byway—also designated as Gogebic County Road 513—runs about 11 miles north from the intersection with County Road 204 in Ironwood Township to Black River Harbor, just before the river empties into Lake Superior.) The 20-foot Great Conglomerate Falls is a recommended destination and is named for the unique conglomerate rock (a rock that contains other small rocks) that forms the base of the falls. Other notable waterfalls on the byway include Gorge Falls (25 feet), Potawatomi Falls (30 feet), Sandstone Falls (15 feet), Rainbow Falls (30 feet), and Gabbro Falls (40 feet). Check the website above for trail lengths and recommended hiking experience levels.

2 Yellow Dog Falls

Northwest of Marquette off County Road 501; (906) 228-4321

tinyurl.com/yellowdogfalls, gowaterfalling.com/waterfalls/yellowdog.shtml

Yellow Dog Falls is approximately 50 feet wide, with a vertical drop of more than 20 feet over several drops. One unique and distinctive feature that photographers enjoy is a huge boulder that sits in the center of the falls and splits the flow in two. To get here you must drive out of town and find the hiking trail on the south side of the river, about a half mile before the bridge. The walking trail is just under 2.5 miles and recommended for more-experienced hikers.

Waterfalls

Morel Mushrooms are the star of the show at Boyne City's Morel Mushroom Festival

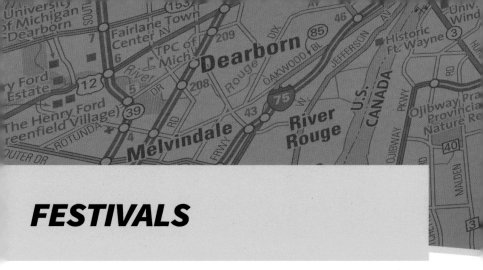

FESTIVALS

NATURE & SCIENCE

Aldo Leopold Festival
(Birding, wildflower, and paddling tours)
Les Cheneaux Islands, June
aldoleopoldfestival.com

Blue Water SandFest
(Michigan's only master-level/advanced-amateur sand-sculpting competition)
Port Huron, August
bluewatersandfest.com

CraneFest
Battle Creek, October
michiganaudubon.org/news-events/signature-events/cranefest, facebook.com
/battlecreekkiwanisclub

Earth Day Festival
Ann Arbor, April
lesliesnc.org/a2earthday

Keewenaw Migratory Bird Festival
Copper Harbor, May
facebook.com/copperharborbirdingandnature

Mayville Sunflower Festival
Mayville, October
mayvillesunflowerfestival.com

Michigan Brown Trout Festival
Alpena, July
browntroutefestival.com

Michigan State University Science Festival
East Lansing, April
sciencefestival.msu.edu

(continued on next page)

National Morel Mushroom Festival
Boyne City, May
bcmorelfestival.com

The Original Michigan Lavender Festival
Imlay City, June
michiganlavenderfestival.net

Petoskey Stone Festival
Eastport, Saturday of Memorial Day weekend (*see profile on page 144*)
petoskeystonefestival.com

Pointe Mouillee Waterfowl Festival
Brownstown, September
ptemouilleewaterfowlfestival.org

Tawas Point Birding Festival
East Tawas, May (*see profile on page 32*)
michiganaudubon.org/calendar/tawas-point-birding-festival-4

Tulip Time Festival
Holland, May (*see profile on page 97*)
tuliptime.com

WINTER FESTIVALS

Downtown Winter Ice Festival
Sault Ste. Marie, February
saultstemarie.com/downtown-winter-ice-festival

Frostbite Winter Festival
Harrison, February
clarecounty.net/frostbite.html

Hunter Ice Festival
Niles, January
nilesmi.org/business/niles_dda_main_street/hunter_ice_festival/index.php

Michigan Tech University Winter Carnival
Houghton, February
mtu.edu/carnival

Plymouth Ice Festival
Plymouth, February
plymouthicefestival.com

Silver Bells in the City
Lansing, Friday before Thanksgiving
silverbellsinthecity.com

Tip-Up Town USA
(Michigan's longest-running winter festival)
Houghton Lake, January
houghtonlakechamber.net/tip-up-town-usa

Holland, Michigan, is practically synonymous with Tulips

Several festivals in Michigan are dedicated to Jazz

ARTS & CULTURE

ARTS & MUSIC

African World Festival
Detroit, August
thewright.org/events/african-world-festival

Alpena Blues Festival
Alpena, summer
alpenablues.org

Ann Arbor Film Festival
Ann Arbor, March
aafilmfest.org

Ann Arbor Folk Festival
Ann Arbor, last weekend in January (*see profile on page 38*)
theark.org/folk-festival

Ann Arbor Summer Festival
Ann Arbor, June–July
a2sf.org

Cinetopia Film Festival
Various locations in metro Detroit and Ann Arbor, spring
cinetopiafestival.org

Concerts in the Park Series
Memorial Park, Frankenmuth, summer
frankenmuthwomensclub.org/concerts-in-the-park

Detroit SheTown Film Festival
Detroit, October
detroitshetownfilmfestival.com

East Lansing Art Festival
East Lansing, usually in May (*see profile on page 39*)
elartfest.com

Frankenmuth Summer Music Fest
Frankenmuth, August
frankenmuthfestivals.com

(continued on next page)

Freep Film Festival
Various locations in downtown and metro Detroit; usually in April
freepfilmfestival.org

Gilda's LaughFest
Grand Rapids, March
laughfestgr.org

Hiawatha Traditional Music Festival
Marquette, July (*see profile on page 41*)
hiawathamusic.org

Irving S. Gilmore International Keyboard Festival
Kalamazoo, April and May (*see profile on page 40*)
thegilmore.org/festival

Jackson Storyfest
Jackson, October
myjdl.com/storyfest

Michigan Jazz Festival
Livonia, July
michiganjazzfestival.org

Michigan State University Arts & Crafts Shows
East Lansing, May and December
uabevents.com/annualartscrafts

Summer Solstice Jazz Festival
East Lansing, June
eljazzfest.com

HERITAGE

Arab and Chaldean Festival
Detroit, July
arabandchaldeanfestival.com

Dozynki Polish Festival
Grand Rapids, last full weekend of August
polishheritagesociety.com

Frankenmuth Bavarian Festival
Frankenmuth, June
bavarianfestival.org

Frankenmuth Oktoberfest
Frankenmuth, fall
frankenmuthfestivals.com

Heikinpäivä: A Midwinter Finnish-American Festival
Hancock, midwinter
finlandia.edu/heikinpaiva, tinyurl.com/heikinpaivafacebook

Irish Festival
Clare, March
clareirishfestival.com

Native American Festival
St. Ignace, May
stignace.com/event/native-american-festival

Opa! Fest
Troy, June
opafest.org

Parade of Nations and International Food Festival
Houghton, September
mtu.edu/international/events-programs/parade-nations

Polish Festival
Bronson, July
bronson-mi.com/about/polish-festival

Pride Festivals (LGBTQ)
(For additional events, search online for "Michigan Pride Festivals.")
Ann Arbor Pride Ann Arbor, August, annarborpride.com

Grand Rapids Pride Grand Rapids, June, grpride.org/festival

LGBT Detroit Pride Detroit, July, lgbtdetroit.org

Michigan Pride Lansing, summer, michiganpride.org

Motor City Pride Detroit, June, motorcitypride.org

Up North Pride Traverse City, June, upnorthpride.com

Saline Celtic Festival
Saline, July
salineceltic.org

A Taste of Greece Festival
Plymouth, last weekend in August
michigangreekfestival.com

Ya'ssoo Greek Festival of Ann Arbor
Ann Arbor, June
annarborgreekfestival.org

Ypsilanti Heritage Festival (YpsiFest)
Ypsilanti, August
ypsifest.com

AGRICULTURE/FOOD & DRINK

Alden Strawberry Festival
Alden, June
visitalden.com/eventsinalden/strawberryfestival.html

Annual Wild Blueberry Festival
Paradise, August
wildblueberryfestival.org

Applefest
Coldwater, September
coldwater.org

(continued on next page)

Art & Apples Festival
Rochester, September
pccart.org/festival

Charlevoix Apple Festival
Charlevoix, October
visitcharlevoix.com/apple-festival

Chase Pickle Festival
Chase, Saturday after Labor Day
facebook.com/chasepicklefestival

Copper Country Strawberry Festival
Chassell, July
coppercountrystrawberryfestival.com/

Elsie Dairy Festival
Elsie, summer
facebook.com/elsiedairyfestival

Empire Asparagus Festival
Empire, May
empirechamber.com/event/asparagus-festival

Festival of the Angry Bear, Ore Dock Brewing Company
Marquette, April
ore-dock.com/events/angry-bear-festival

Four Flags Area Apple Festival
Niles, October; fourflagsapplefestival.org

Giant Pumpkin Festival
Menominee, September
facebook.com/giantpumpkinfestival

Hanover-Horton Maple Syrup Festival
Hanover, Third Saturday in March
conklinreedorganmuseum.org/park.htm

Howell Melon Festival
Howell, summer
howellmelonfestival.com

Mackinac Island Fudge Festival
Mackinac Island, August
mackinacisland.org/mackinac-island-fudge-festival

Marquette Blueberry Festival
Marquette, last Friday in July
downtownmarquette.org/downtown-events/blueberry-festival

Michigan Apple Fest
Sparta, September
michiganapplefest.com

Michigan Beer and Brat Festival
Thompsonville, May
crystalmountain.com/event/beerfest

Montrose Blueberry Festival
Montrose, August
montroseblueberryfestival.net

National Asparagus Festival
Oceana County, summer
nationalasparagusfestival.org

National Blueberry Festival
South Haven, second weekend in August
blueberryfestival.com

National Cereal Festival
Battle Creek, June
battlecreeklive.com/cerealfest

National Cherry Festival
Traverse City, summer
cherryfestival.org

National Strawberry Festival
Belleville, Father's Day weekend
nationalstrawberryfest.com

Romeo Peach Festival, Romeo
Labor Day weekend; romeopeachfestival.com

Romulus DDA Pumpkin Festival
Romulus, begins third Friday in September
romulusgov.com/pumpkinfestival

Tecumseh Appleumpkin Festival
Tecumseh, fall
downtowntecumseh.com/events/october

Tuscola County Pumpkin Festival
Caro, first weekend in October
tuscolacountypumpkinfestival.com

Vermontville Maple Syrup Festival
Vermontville, last full weekend in April
vermontvillemaplesyrupfestival.org

World Expo of Beer
Frankenmuth, May
worldexpoofbeer.com

MISCELLANEOUS

Cheeseburger in Caseville
Caseville, August
casevillechamber.org

Frankenmuth Dog Bowl
Frankenmuth, May; dogbowlfun.com

March Mannequins
(Local volunteers pose as "mannequins" in storefront window displays.)
Saint Joseph, March
stjoetoday.com/marchmannequins

Michigan International Alpaca Fest
Dimondale, October
facebook.com/michiganinternationalalpacafest

Cherries and Michigan go hand-in-hand

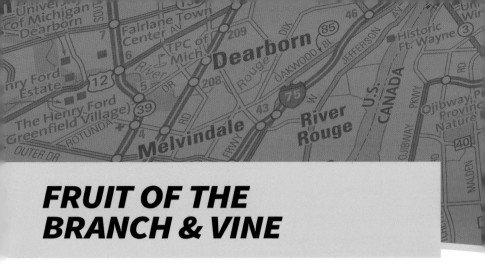

FRUIT OF THE BRANCH & VINE

ORCHARDS & U-PICK FARMS

For additional listings organized by region, see pickyourown.org/MI.htm.

Blake's Orchard & Cider Mill
17985 Armada Center Road, Armada 48005; (586) 784-5343
blakefarms.com/venue/orchard-cider-mill

Buchan's Blueberry Hill
1472 Nelson Road, Traverse City 49686; (231) 223-4846 (hours vary, so call before visiting)
buchansblueberryhill.com

Crane Orchards
6054 124th Ave., Fennville 49408; (269) 561-8651
craneorchards.com

Dexter Cider Mill
3685 Central St., Dexter 48130; no phone
dextercidermill.com

Diehl's Orchard
1479 Ranch Road, Holly 48442; (248) 634-8981
diehlsorchard.com

Franklin Cider Mill
7450 Franklin Road, Bloomfield Hills 48301; (248) 626-8261
franklincidermill.com

Fruit Acres Farm Market and U-Pick
Farm Market 3452 Friday Road, Coloma 49038; (269) 468-3668

Cherry U-Pick 6299 Carmody Road, Coloma 49038; (269) 208-3591

Peach and Apple U-Pick 2789 Friday Road, Coloma 49038; (269) 208-3591
fruiteacresfarm.com

(continued on next page)

Historic Yates Cider Mill
1990 E. Avon Road, Rochester Hills 48307; (248) 651-8300
yatescidermill.com

King Orchards
4629 N. M-88, Central Lake 49622; (231) 544-6479
kingorchards.com

Overhiser Orchards
6405 109th Ave., South Haven 49090; (269) 236-6312
overhiserorchards.com

Rennie Orchards
11221 Munro Road, Williamsburg 49690; (231) 264-8387, (231) 313-7847
rennieorchards.com

Robinette's Apple Haus & Winery
3142 Four Mile Road NE, Grand Rapids 49525; (800) 400-8100
robinettes.com

Royal Farms Farm Market & Winery
10445 US 31 N., Ellsworth 49729; (231) 599-3222
royalfarmsinc.com

Spicer Orchards
10411 Clyde Road, Fenton 48430; (810) 632-7692
spicerorchards.com

VINEYARDS & WINERIES

Also see "Beer, Wine, and Spirits Trails & Tours," page 105.

Bonobo Winery
12011 Center Road, Traverse City 49686; (231) 282-9463
bonobowinery.com

Chateau Aeronautique Winery
1849 Rives Eaton Road, Jackson 49201; (517) 569-2132
chateauaeronautiquewinery.com

Ciccone Vineyard & Winery
10343 E. Hilltop Road, Suttons Bay 49682; (231) 271-5553
cicconevineyard.com

Fenn Valley Vineyards
6130 122nd Ave., Fennville 49408; (269) 561-2396
fennvalley.com

Lake Michigan Vintners
2774 E. Empire Ave., Benton Harbor 49022; (269) 927-4731
lakemichiganvintners.com

Lemon Creek Winery
533 E. Lemon Creek Road, Berrien Springs 49103; (269) 471-1321
lemoncreekwinery.com

St. Julian Winery
716 S. Kalamazoo St., Paw Paw 49079; (800) 732-6002
stjulian.com

Tabor Hill Winery & Restaurant
185 Mt. Tabor Road, Buchanan 49107; (269) 422-1161
taborhill.com

2 Lads Winery
16985 Smokey Hollow Road, Traverse City 49686; (231) 223-7722
2lwinery.com

Grapes in Michigan's Wine Country

Tiger statues on display at Tiger Stadium

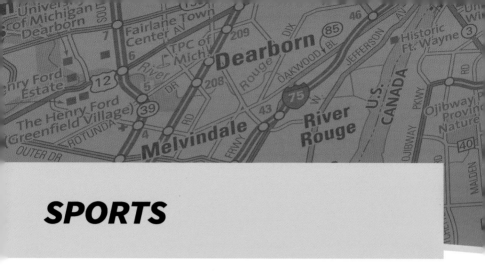

SPORTS

BASEBALL

MAJOR LEAGUE BASEBALL
Detroit Tigers
Comerica Park, 2100 Woodward Ave., Detroit 48201; (313) 962-4000
detroittigers.com

MINOR LEAGUE BASEBALL
Great Lakes Loons
Dow Diamond, 825 E. Main St., Midland 48640; (989) 837-2255
milb.com/great-lakes

Lansing Lugnuts
Jackson Field, 505 E. Michigan Ave., Lansing 48912; (517) 485-4500
milb.com/lansing

Western Michigan Whitecaps
LMCU Ballpark, 4500 W. River Drive, Comstock Park 49321; (616) 784-4131
milb.com/west-michigan

BASKETBALL

NATIONAL BASKETBALL ASSOCIATION
Detroit Pistons
Little Caesars Arena, 2645 Woodward Ave., Detroit 48201; (313) 471-7000
nba.com/pistons

NBA G LEAGUE
Grand Rapids Drive
DeltaPlex Arena & Conference Center, 2500 Turner Ave. NW, Grand Rapids 49544; (616) 364-9000
grandrapids.gleague.nba.com

Motor City Cruise
Motor City Cruise Arena, Wayne State University, Detroit 48202; (313) 747-8667
nba.com/pistons/tickets/g-league-detroit

(continued on next page)

FOOTBALL

NATIONAL FOOTBALL LEAGUE

Detroit Lions

Ford Field, 2000 Brush St., Detroit 48226; (313) 262-2008
detroitlions.com

WOMEN'S FOOTBALL ALLIANCE

Detroit Dark Angels

MacArthur K–8 University Academy, 19301 W. 12 Mile Road, Lathrup Village 48076;
(248) 413-5236
detroitdarkangels.com

Ford Field, home of the Detroit Lions

HOCKEY

AMERICAN HOCKEY LEAGUE
Grand Rapids Griffins
Van Andel Arena, 130 Fulton St. W., Grand Rapids 49503; (616) 774-4585
griffinshockey.com

ECHL
Kalamazoo Wings
Wings Event Center, 3600 Vanrick Drive, Kalamazoo 49001; (269) 226-0388
kwings.com

FEDERAL PROSPECTS HOCKEY LEAGUE
Port Huron Prowlers
McMorran Place, 701 McMorran Blvd., Port Huron 48060; (810) 966-0396
phprowlers.com

NATIONAL HOCKEY LEAGUE
Detroit Red Wings
Little Caesars Arena, 2645 Woodward Ave., Detroit 48201; (313) 471-7000
nhl.com/redwings

ONTARIO HOCKEY LEAGUE
Flint Firebirds
Dort Financial Center, 3501 Lapeer Road, Flint 48503; (810) 742-2004
flintfirebirds.com

Saginaw Spirit
Dow Event Center, 303 Johnson St., Saginaw 48607; (989) 497-7747
saginawspirit.com

SOCCER

MAJOR ARENA SOCCER LEAGUE 2
Detroit Waza Flo
Taylor Sportsplex, 13333 Telegraph Road, Taylor 48180; (303) 709-4744
wazaflo.soccershift.com

Muskegon Risers
Mercy Health Arena, 470 W. Western Ave., Muskegon 49440; (231) 299-0006
muskegonrisers.com

NATIONAL INDEPENDENT SOCCER ASSOCIATION
Detroit City Football Club
Keyworth Stadium, 3201 Roosevelt St., Hamtramck 48212; (313) 656-2480
detcityfc.com

Michigan Stars Football Club
Michigan Stars Sports Center, 65665 Powell Road, Washington 48095;
(586) 488-7161
michiganstarsfc.com

NATIONAL PREMIER SOCCER LEAGUE
Carpathia Football Club
Avondale High School, 2800 Waukegan St., Auburn Hills 48326; (586) 978-2292
carpathiafc.com

(continued on next page)

Sports

USL TWO (United Soccer League)
AFC Ann Arbor
Concordia University Stadium, 283 Earhart Road, Ann Arbor 48105; (734) 408-1627
afcannarbor.com

Flint City Bucks
Atwood Stadium, Kettering University, 701 University Ave., Flint 48503;
(810) 666-2515; flintcitybucks.com

Grand Rapids Football Club
Houseman Field, 162 Houseman Ave. NE, Grand Rapids 49503; (616) 234-4000
grandrapidsfc.com

Kalamazoo Football Club
Mayors' Riverfront Park, 251 Mills St., Kalamazoo 49408; (269) 337-8191
kalamazoofc.com

Oakland County Football Club
Clawson Stadium, 935 N. Custer Ave., Clawson 48017; (248) 629-0251
oaklandcountyfc.com

UNITED WOMEN'S SOCCER
Corktown AFC
The Corner Ballpark, 1680 Michigan Ave., Detroit 48216; (313) 274-8500
corktownafc.com

Detroit City Football Club
Keyworth Stadium, 3201 Roosevelt St., Hamtramck 48212; (313) 656-2480
detcityfc.com

Lansing United
East Lansing Soccer Complex, 3700 Coleman Road, East Lansing 48823;
(517) 319-6809; launited.com

Midwest United Football Club
Aquinas College, 1700 Fulton St. E., Grand Rapids 49506; (616) 920-0113
midwestunitedfc.com, midwestunitedfcwomen.com

Muskegon Risers
Mercy Health Arena, 470 W. Western Ave., Muskegon 49440; (231) 299-0006
muskegonrisers.com

COLLEGIATE SPORTS

NCAA DIVISION I
Central Michigan Chippewas
Central Michigan University, Mount Pleasant; tickets: (888) 347-3872
cmuchippewas.com

Detroit Mercy Titans
University of Detroit Mercy, Detroit; tickets: (313) 993-1700, ext. 7301
detroittitans.com

Eastern Michigan Eagles
Eastern Michigan University, Ypsilanti; tickets: (734) 487-3669
emueagles.com

Michigan State Spartans

Michigan State University, East Lansing; tickets: (800) 467-8283
msuspartans.com

Michigan Wolverines

University of Michigan, Ann Arbor; tickets: (866) 296-6849
mgoblue.com

Oakland Golden Grizzlies

Oakland University, Rochester; tickets: (248) 370-4000
goldengrizzlies.com

Western Michigan Broncos

Western Michigan University, Kalamazoo; tickets: (888) 496-8849
wmubroncos.com

NCAA DIVISION II*

Davenport Panthers

Davenport University, Grand Rapids; tickets: (800) 514-3849
dupanthers.com

Ferris State Bulldogs

Ferris State University, Big Rapids; tickets: (800) 585-3737
ferrisstatebulldogs.com

Grand Valley State Lakers

Grand Valley State University, Allendale; tickets: (616) 331-3200
gvsulakers.com

Hillsdale Chargers

Hillsdale College, Hillsdale; (517) 437-7364
hillsdalechargers.com; tickets: hillsdale.universitytickets.com

Lake Superior State Lakers

Lake Superior State University, Sault Ste. Marie; (906) 635-2601
lssulakers.com, tickets: lssulakerstickets.universitytickets.com

Michigan Tech Huskies

Michigan Tech University, Houghton; tickets: (906) 487-2073
michigantechhuskies.com

Northern Michigan Wildcats

Northern Michigan University, Marquette; tickets: (906) 227-1032
nmuwildcats.com

Northwood Timberwolves

Northwood University, Midland; tickets: (989) 837-4381
timberwolves.gonorthwood.com

Saginaw Valley State Cardinals

Saginaw Valley State University, University Center; tickets: (989) 964-4348
svsucardinals.com

Wayne State Warriors

Wayne State University, Detroit; tickets: (313) 577-2779
wsuathletics.com
The men's hockey teams at Ferris State, Lake Superior State, Michigan Tech, and Northern Michigan Universities compete in NCAA Division I as members of the Central Collegiate Hockey Association.

Index

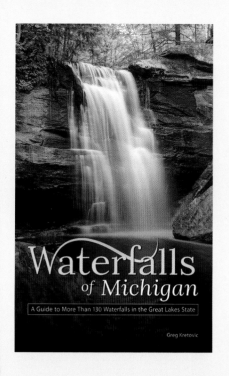

Waterfalls of Michigan

Greg Kretovic

ISBN: 978-1-59193-771-5 • **$14.95** • **6 x 9** • **paperback**
232 pages • **full-color photos**

Professional photographer and Michigan native Greg Kretovic guides you to Michigan's top-ranked waterfalls. They are organized geographically and ranked by beauty. Entries include all the information you need, like directions and hike difficulty, as well as details about each waterfall, such as the best time to visit. Nearby activities are also called out, so you can make the most of every outing. Plus, Greg's incomparable photography makes this guidebook worthy of any coffee table. These natural wonders prove that the Great Lake State is home to some of the most picturesque sites in America!

Little Michigan: A Nostalgic Look at Michigan's Smallest Towns

Kathryn Houghton

ISBN: 978-1-59193-768-5 • $16.95 • 9.75 x 8 • paperback
240 pages • full-color photos

Little Michigan presents 100 towns with populations under 600. With full-color photographs, fun facts, and fascinating details about every locale, it's almost as if you're walking down Main Street, waving hello to folks who know all of their neighbors. The locations featured in this book range from quaint to historic, and they wonderfully represent the Great Lakes State. Little Michigan is for anyone who grew up in a small town and for everyone who takes pride in being called a Michigander. They may be small towns, but they have huge character!

The Veteran's Memorial at Boyne Falls, Michigan

About the Authors

Born and raised in mid-Michigan, **Kathryn Houghton** has spent most of her life in the Mitten State. She can't imagine living anywhere else, and not just because no one in Michigan looks at her funny when she calls soft drinks pop instead of soda. Kathryn, who lives in Holt with her sister and three dogs, teaches writing and editing at Michigan State University. She is also the author of *Little Michigan: A Nostalgic Look at Michigan's Smallest Towns* (Adventure Publications).

Mike Link and **Kate Crowley** were the authors of the first two editions of this book. Mike is the author of many books, a speaker, and a wilderness guide. He and his wife, Kate Crowley, walked around the entire shoreline of Lake Superior—the only couple to ever do so—and they plan to bike the length of the Mississippi River next.